The
Siberian Iris

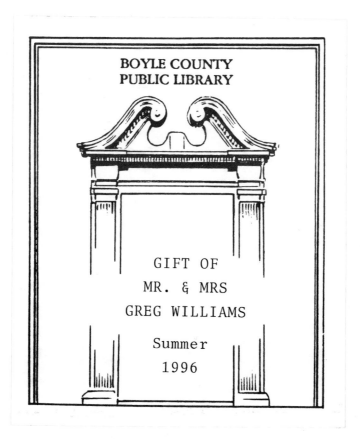

The Siberian Iris

Currier McEwen

with illustrations by
Jean G. Witt

Timber Press
Portland, Oregon

ISBN 0-88192-329-X

Printed in Hong Kong

TIMBER PRESS, INC.
The Haseltine Building
133 S.W. Second Avenue, Suite 450
Portland, Oregon 97204, U.S.A.

Library of Congress Cataloging-in-Publication Data

McEwen, Currier.
    The Siberian Iris / Currier McEwen ; with illustrations by
Jean G. Witt.
        p.   cm.
    Includes bibliographical references (p.   ) and indexes.
    ISBN 0-88192-329-X
    1. Siberian iris.   I. Title.   2. Iris
    SB413.I8M275   1996
    635.9'3424–dc20   4 0s   94-14643
                                                               CIP

To
Peg Edwards,
founder of the Society for Siberian Irises,
and
Fred W. Cassebeer and William G. McGarvey,
pioneers in the development of the modern siberian irises

Contents

Color plates follow page 36

Preface

This book was written with the encouragement of the Society for Siberian Irises and the expert assistance of the consultants whose names follow. Each chapter was reviewed by three or more of those friends whose judgment I especially trusted for a particular chapter. As a result, I am confident that discussion of the various topics is as correct and complete as I can make it in the light of current knowledge. Furthermore, these advisors are widely scattered from east to west and north to south, and thus their experience provides firsthand knowledge of growing conditions in most places where readers of this book may live.

The help of all these friends is most gratefully acknowledged. Particular thanks go to Jean Witt for her superb watercolors of the species and pen-and-ink drawings. I must thank her, Anne Blanco White, Leroy Davidson, Jennifer Hewitt, and James Waddick for much information regarding the chapters on history and on the species. Judith Hollingworth and Sarah Tiffney never failed to answer the many wide-ranging questions I put to them. Robert Hollingworth was a constant source of help for the chapters on pests and diseases, and he, Ben Hager, and Martin Schafer for the chapter on culture. I leaned heavily on Anna Mae Miller, Janet Sacks, and Barbara Schmieder for details on iris shows and on the uses of siberian irises in the garden and in arrangements. Kay Nelson-Keppel and Kenneth Waite were particularly helpful regarding awards and registration. William Ackerman and Tomas Tamberg provided expert advice for the discussion of wide-cross hybrids, and Chandler Fulton and

Donald Koza for that of gene transfer. Chandler Fulton also read the entire manuscript and offered many useful suggestions. I am indebted to the friends who generously provided slides for the color plates. The chapter on siberian irises in other countries was made possible by the information kindly provided by the many in those countries who responded to my requests for assistance.

Thanks go to Hubbard C. Goodrich for his scholarly and careful assistance in the preparation of the manuscript.

Consultants

Ellen and Thomas Abrego, Newberg, Oregon
Dr. William L. Ackerman, Ashton, Maryland
Dr. Edward H. Ahrens, Jr., Bronxville, New York
Terry Aitken, Vancouver, Washington
Robert A. Bauer, Galesburg, Michigan
Mrs. T. A. (Anne) Blanco White, London, Britain
Howard L. Brookins, Menomonee Falls, Wisconsin
Mrs. Wells E. (Virginia) Burton, Summerville, South Carolina
John A. Coble, Galesburg, Michigan
Leroy Davidson, Bellevue, Washington
Koen Engelen, Ranst, Belgium
Drs. Elaine and Chandler Fulton, Weston, Massachusetts
Ben R. Hager, Stockton, California
Mrs. Jennifer Hewitt, Kidderminster, Britain
Mrs. Judith and Dr. Robert Hollingworth, Williamston, Michigan
Akira Horinaka, Nishinomiya, Japan
Toyokazi Ichie, Kakagawa, Japan
Mototeru Kamo, Kakagawa, Japan
Dr. Donald W. Koza, St. Paul, Minnesota
Dr. Lee Lenz, Claremont, California
Mrs. Ronald F. (Anna Mae) Miller, Kalamazoo, Michigan
Mrs. Kathleen Nelson-Keppel, Salem, Oregon [deceased]
Mrs. Maurice B. (Shirley) Pope, Gorham, Maine
Mrs. Lorena M. Reid, Springfield, Oregon
Allan L. Rogers, Sherwood, Oregon
Dr. George I. Rodionenko, St. Petersburg, Russia
Janet Sacks and Martin Schafer, Carlisle, Massachusetts
Barbara and David Schmieder, Concord, Massachusetts

Hiroshi Shimizu, Sagamihara, Japan
Dr. Tomas Tamberg, Berlin, Germany
Mrs. Wesley N. (Sarah) Tiffney, Sharon, Massachusetts
Mrs. Joan Trevithick, Radcliff-on-Trent, Britain [deceased]
Steve Varner, Monticello, Illinois
Dr. Kevin C. Vaughn, Stoneville, Mississippi
Dr. James W. Waddick, Kansas City, Missouri
Julius Wadekamper, Faribault, Minnesota
Kenneth M. Waite, Westfield, Massachusetts
Mrs. Andrew C. (Carol) Warner, Upperco, Maryland
Evelyn and John White, Minot, Maine
Mrs. Sharon Hayes Whitney, South Harpswell, Maine
Mrs. Jean G. Witt, Seattle, Washington

Chapter 1

History

The beautiful plants known as siberian irises include and are derived from the eleven species of series *Sibiricae* of the genus *Iris*. Although bearded irises were known as early as the 6th century, the earliest mention of what was surely a siberian iris came, I believe, nine centuries later, in a treatise by Carolus Clusius. In all the intervening centuries and, indeed, well into the 17th century, plants were grown and studied not as botanical subjects nor as garden flowers but as sources of medicines. The herbalists have left many quaint records of plants and how to prepare them as medicines to be given to the patient, often "sodden wyth wyne." The medicinal virtues attributed to irises were truly remarkable; among other benefits, iris decoctions were believed to remove freckles, induce sleep, and cure ulcers and gynecological complaints (Dykes 1913; Davidson 1992).

Against this background, the French physician-botanist Charles de L'Écluse (1526–1609) stands out in sharp contrast. The treatises he wrote under the name Carolus Clusius in 1576 and 1583 and his *Rariorum Plantarum Historia*, printed in Antwerp in 1601, show his interest in and knowledge of plants as garden subjects. Among the species of irises he named were several he called *Iris angustifolia*. His detailed descriptions of plants he included under that name show that one, *I. angustifolia media*, was the species now named *I. sibirica* L. By 1600 *I. angustifolia media* was growing in the Chelsea Physic Garden in London, England, which still exists as an example of the apothecary collections of those days (Davidson 1992).

In his famous *Species Plantarum* published in 1753, Carl Linnaeus uses the name *Iris sibirica* for the species called since then by that name. This species grows in central Europe, as Clusius—who collected it in Austria—knew. It is not native to Siberia, but the somewhat similar *I. sanguinea* is. Linnaeus did not have firsthand knowledge of the plant he called *I. sibirica* but took the name from Johann G. Gmelin, who had studied the plants of Siberia. One can assume that Gmelin described as *I. sibirica* the iris growing there, namely the one now known as *I. sanguinea*. Herbarium specimens show that *I. sanguinea* was known in Europe by the second half of the 18th century. Apparently Linnaeus confused the two species. Although geographically misleading, the name *I. sibirica* is universally accepted, and indeed, its name has been adopted for the entire series *Sibiricae*.

The second species to be described was *Iris sanguinea*. It was named *I. orientalis* by Carl Peter Thunberg in 1794 and was widely known by that name until the 1950s. Meanwhile botanists had discovered that the name *I. orientalis* had been given, prior to 1794, to an iris species of series *Spuriae*. According to the rules governing taxonomic nomenclature, the name *I. orientalis* was therefore invalid for any other iris, and the name *I. sanguinea*, given to it by James Donn in 1811, has been accepted as correct. This name was used in various publications, including *Garden Irises* (published by the American Iris Society in 1959), and gradually became the name in general use. Although not botanically described until 1894, this species was cultivated in Japan as early as 1681. In 1882 the firm of Krelage in Holland listed it in their catalog, but it was little known in the West until 1900, when Peter Barr introduced it in England (Davidson 1989).

The next species to be recognized was *Iris clarkei*. Plants of this species were sketched growing in the wild as early as 1848 by Joseph Dalton Hooker, but it was not collected until 1875, when Charles Baron Clarke discovered it near Darjeeling in the Himalaya Mountains. It was subsequently described and named in Clarke's honor by John Gilbert Baker, in 1892. This was at the start of the important period when many plants previously unknown in the West were discovered in China and other points East by professional collectors, missionaries, and others, who sent specimens back to friends and sponsors in the home countries. This interest in collecting new plants was especially keen in Britain.

The four other well-accepted species of siberian irises were also recognized in this period. *Iris delavayi* was named by Marc Micheli in 1895 to honor Abbé Pierre Jean Marie Delavay, who had discovered it in Sichuan in 1884. In 1907 Ernest H. Wilson, who was collecting plants in China for the English firm of Veitch and Sons, collected the yellow species subsequently named *I. wilsonii* in his honor by Charles H. Wright. Similarly, *I. forrestii* was collected by George Forrest in the Lichiang Mountains in Yunnan Province and was named for him by William Rickatson Dykes in 1910. The fourth, *I. chrysographes*, was discovered in Sichuan by Wilson in 1908 and was described and named by Dykes in 1911.

Three additional species have been included among the siberian irises. They are *Iris bulleyana*, named by Dykes in 1910; *I. phragmitetorum*, collected by Heinrich Handel-Mazzetti in 1916; and *I. dykesii*, named by Otto Stapf in 1926. The status of these as true species has long been questioned. This is discussed in more detail in Chapter 3.

Since the naming of these ten species, botanists have speculated that other irises belonging to the siberian group might exist, and indeed, one more has been identified. The Japanese botanist Masao Kitagawa discovered a previously undescribed iris in extreme northeast China in 1934. Because its narrow, slightly twisted leaves somewhat resemble those of cattails (or reedmaces, as they are known in Britain), Kitagawa named it *Iris typhifolia* after *Typha*, the genus to which cattails belong (Kitagawa 1939, 1979). In spite of Kitagawa's discovery, *I. typhifolia* was not known in the West until the late 1980s, when Zhao Yu-tang, the leading authority on irises in China, rediscovered it in remote areas of Nei Menggu (Inner Mongolia), Liaoning, and Jilin Provinces and obtained plants and seeds, which he distributed to iris growers in Britain, France, and Germany. *Iris typhifolia* has since become rather widely known and has attracted much interest (Berlin 1989; Wise 1990; Waddick 1991; Waddick and Zhao 1992).

In the 1920s and '30s, as the various species became available, hybridizers began using them for crosses and a large number of interspecies and even interseries hybrids resulted. This breeding effort was carried out especially in Britain, where Dykes, Amos Perry, and Robert W. Wallace attempted crosses not only between all the then-known siberian iris species but also between species of series *Sibiricae* and species of other series, particularly those of series *Californicae*. Dykes was the first to report successful crosses of the *Californicae* with *Iris clarkei*, *I. wilsonii*, and *I. chrysographes*. Perry continued Dykes's program and produced many of these interseries hybrids, including 'Margot Holmes', the first English Dykes Medal winner.

Aside from the species, seventeen cultivars of siberian irises were recorded by 1900. Most, if not all, were selected examples of *Iris sibirica* or *I. sanguinea*; a few may have been hybrids resulting from naturally occurring crosses between these two species. Almost certainly none was the result of a planned cross. The first may have been *I. sibirica* 'Alba', illustrated in *Curtis's Botanical Magazine* in 1809. Unfortunately, the pioneer who named it remains anonymous, and although several examples of white *I. sibirica* exist, this cultivar is no longer known. The miniature *I. sibirica* 'Acuta', named only four years later by Karl Ludwig Willdenow, is still available. By 1852 three more were named, including *I. sibirica* 'Flore Pleno', which must have had double flowers to be so called. Twenty years passed before the next cultivar was named. From 1872 to 1900 only eleven new siberian irises were recorded, three of which are still available: 'Nigrescens', named by Louis Benart Van Houtte; 'George Wallace', by Robert W. Wallace; and 'Snow Queen', a white form of *I. sanguinea*, by Peter Barr. The pleasing forms of 'Snow Queen', brought to England from the Orient in 1900, and its blue counterpart 'Emperor', introduced by Barr fourteen years later, played an especially important role in arousing early interest in siberian irises.

For several subsequent decades, no dramatic developments occurred, but many excellent cultivars were introduced. Frances Cleveland registered some forty siberian irises between 1920 and 1938, including her large blue 'Tycoon' and the still much-loved 'Summer Sky'. Elizabeth Scheffy registered ten between 1944 and 1953, every one excellent in its day and all still fine examples of the traditional form. Her 'Fairy Dawn' is in the background of many lavender-pinks, and her 'My Love' was the first repeat bloomer to be recognized and remains one of the most reliable and best. Other superior introductions of that period included L. Merton Gage's 'Snowcrest' and Fred R. Whitney's 'Eric the Red'. In England, Marjorie Brummitt's outstanding hybridizing efforts resulted in such excellent cultivars as 'Anniversary' and 'Limeheart' (white), 'Dreaming Spires' (dark blue), and the lovely 'Cambridge' (lighter blue). Other important English hybridizers of that period were Philip J. Hutchinson and Maurice Kitton.

Siberian iris check lists document that by 1975, 590 siberian irises were named by 123 different breeders and collectors. Most of these cultivars involved *Iris sibirica* and *I. sanguinea*. Fewer than 100 came from the other eight species, and only eighteen were interseries hybrids (McEwen 1976). Since 1975, the number of new registrations each year has steadily increased and now reaches thirty to fifty annually.

Until the 1950s, most named siberian irises were seedlings from natural crosses, with neither or only one parent known. Since then and only gradually, planned crosses have become the rule, although some seedlings from unplanned crosses continue to be named each year. In 1990, for example, of the fifty siberian irises registered by the American Iris Society, both parents are known for 70 percent, only the pod parent for 20 percent, and neither parent for 10 percent.

Isabella Preston was a pioneer in making planned crosses. Trained in England at the Royal Botanic Gardens, Kew, she went on to become a staff member of the Dominion Experiment Station in Ottawa, Canada. All but four of the nineteen cultivars she named came from planned, protected crosses. The most important of these was 'Gatineau', from a cross of *Iris sibirica* 'Maxima' and *I. sanguinea* 'Snow Queen', registered in 1930. It was the closest to true blue in its day and was used a great deal by later hybridizers. Another important figure of that period was F. Cleveland Morgan of Montreal, Canada. Using *I. sibirica* 'Nigrescens' and *I. sanguinea* 'Blue King', he obtained his beautiful dark blue-violet 'Caesar's Brother', which was widely used subsequently as a parent. The Morgan-Wood Medal—the highest award given by the American Iris Society specifically to siberian irises—bears his name.

A most important development in the history of siberian irises occurred in 1957, with the introduction of Fred W. Cassebeer's lovely 'White Swirl' (Plate 12). Its attractive round, flaring form immediately set a standard of excellence for hybridizers and judges. Nearly every siberian iris introduced since 1960 has 'White Swirl' in its background. The late William G. McGarvey, the outstanding hybridizer of siberian irises in the 1960s and '70s, set the lead in using 'White Swirl' as a parent with his own magnificent seedlings, and his beautiful introductions have enriched the gene pool for hybridizers ever since.

The late 1950s saw a return of interest in the interseries crosses first made by Dykes, Wallace, and Perry some thirty years earlier. An article by Lee Lenz (1959) and a chance seedling in a neighboring garden aroused the interest of Jean Witt, who began seriously to cross species of series *Californicae* with species of series *Sibiricae*, such as *Iris chrysographes* and *I. forrestii* (Witt 1959, 1971b, 1978). She was soon joined in these efforts by Lorena Reid and later by Tomas Tamberg (1980). Another major development occurred in the 1960s, with my introduction of tetraploidy in siberian irises (McEwen 1966).

Since the 1960s, interest in siberian irises has increased steadily, and new and improved cultivars are introduced each year by a growing number of hybridizers. Very active societies specifically concerned with siberian irises have been established in the United States and Britain. The journals they publish and the enthusiasm of their members contribute in a very important way to the popularity of these flowers. One can look forward to ever-increasing interest in siberian irises and the creation of many ever-more-beautiful flowers.

Chapter 2

Classification

Irises are of many kinds: bearded and beardless, rhizomatous and bulbous, to mention the major types. From the earliest days of their specialized studies, botanists realized the importance of placing plants with similar or related features in orderly groups. Individual botanists proposed classifications that underwent many modifications over the years.

Before further discussion of the classification of series *Sibiricae*, it will be useful to review briefly the rules governing the use of terms. Since irises are named and assigned to various categories in many different countries, international rules have been developed. A single set of rules, the *International Code of Nomenclature for Cultivated Plants*, governs all horticultural names (Brickell 1980).

The name of an iris species consists of two words and hence is called a binomial. The first word is the name of the genus and the second is the specific name. Both are in Latin or latinized form and, in accordance with the rules, are italicized. The genus name is capitalized, the species name is not, as in *Iris sibirica*. Plants are grouped into hierarchical categories; the names of the categories themselves are given in modern language and are not capitalized or italicized: for example, "kingdom," "family," "section," "genus," "subspecies," and so on. In contrast, the word that follows and defines the category is in Latin or latinized form and is capitalized. If at a level above genus, it is not italicized but rather appears in roman type (e.g., family Iridaceae). If at the level of genus or below, it is italicized (e.g., series *Sibiricae*).

According to international rules, the name first given to a species has priority over any names proposed subsequently. To avoid uncertainty, the name of the person who gave the species its particular name is often written after the binomial, not italicized and frequently abbreviated: for example, *Iris sibirica* L. (for Carl Linnaeus) and *I. delavayi* Mich. (for Marc Micheli). This citing of the botanist's name is customary in botanical writing but is usually omitted in informal horticultural articles.

The naming of individual cultivated varieties also follows international rules, but before considering them, the term "variety" needs definition because it has two different meanings and has therefore been the source of much confusion. In the strictest botanical sense, the term "variety" refers to a group of individual plants within a species that differ sufficiently from the rest of the species' population to be distinguished and given a Latin varietal name. More commonly, it has been used to refer to a cultivated plant that a hybridizer or grower deems worthy of being named. To avoid confusion, a single international term has been adopted for such cultivated varieties, namely "cultivar." By international regulation, cultivar names must not be in Latin or latinized form and are not italicized. The name is capitalized and is enclosed in single quotation marks (e.g., 'White Swirl').

It is essential that there be an official agency charged with responsibility to approve or disapprove all proposed names, to ensure that a given name is used for only one cultivar. The American Iris Society serves as this responsible agency for irises in the United States and other countries.

The starting point for modern plant classification was Carl Linnaeus's *Species Plantarum* in 1753; in it, he included eighteen species of irises. In 1817 the Austrian botanist Leopold Trattinick prepared the first modern classification of irises. Edouard Spach's *Revisio Generis Iris* appeared about 1847 and Friedrich Alefeld's *Revisio Iridearum* in 1866. John Gilbert Baker of the Royal Botanic Gardens, Kew, studied irises intensively and proposed several classifications of them reflecting his changing opinions. In 1913 William Rickatson Dykes published his classic book *The Genus Iris*; he placed nine beardless species in what he called the *sibirica* group, namely *Iris sibirica*, *I. orientalis*, *I. clarkei*, *I. delavayi*, *I. wilsonii*, *I. forrestii*, *I. bulleyana*, *I. chrysographes*, and *I. prismatica* (Dykes 1913). George H. M. Lawrence revised and updated Dykes's classification in 1953, in accordance with the *International Code of Nomenclature for Cultivated Plants*. Lawrence's series *Sibiricae* differed from that of Dykes:

he removed *I. prismatica* to a separate series and added two new species: *I. dykesii* and *I. phragmitetorum* (Lawrence 1953). As explained in Chapter 1, *I. orientalis* later became known as *I. sanguinea*.

Lawrence's classification was adopted by the American Iris Society and is used in the chapters on classification in *Garden Irises* (American Iris Society 1959) and *The World of Irises* (American Iris Society 1978). Subsequently, Brian Mathew modified the Lawrence classification, and since the original 1981 publication of his book *The Iris*, his classification has been rather generally followed (Mathew 1990).

Mathew divides the genus *Iris* into six major groups, called subgenera, which differ quite markedly from each other. Two of these—subgenus *Iris* (the bearded irises) and subgenus *Limniris* (the beardless irises)—contain species distinguished by well-developed rhizomatous rootstocks. The subgenus we are concerned with, subgenus *Limniris*, contains all the beardless and crested species and falls into two groups called sections: section *Lophiris* (the evansia, or crested, irises) and section *Limniris*. Continuing the subdivision, section *Limniris* is further split into sixteen groups called series. The fifth of these, series *Sibiricae*, is the subject of this book.

The classifications of Dykes, Lawrence, Mathew, and George I. Rodionenko (1961) place all species of siberian irises in a single series *Sibiricae*. As the species became available in the West and were crossed with one another, it was found that some crossed readily whereas others were quite incompatible. With the advent of cytogenetics and chromosome counts, the reason became clear. Two members of the series, *Iris sibirica* and *I. sanguinea*, have twenty-eight chromosomes in each somatic (body) cell; all the other species have forty. The two species with twenty-eight chromosomes intercross readily with each other, as do the species with forty chromosomes, but crosses between the two groups are very rarely successful. On the basis of these differences in chromosome numbers, Marc Simonet (1934, 1951) proposed dividing the ten species into two series: the two species with twenty-eight chromosomes in a series *Sibiricae* and the species with forty chromosomes in a series *Chrysographes*.

Over the next few decades, growers of siberian irises began to coin names for the two groups, but the multiplicity of variants was confusing. In 1972 the Society for Siberian Irises appointed a committee on nomenclature to study the differences between the two groups and to propose names that might be consistently used for them (McEwen 1974b). Morphologic features of the species of the two groups were closely observed by members of the committee. Although in general the features are similar, a few discernible differences can be noted. The most obvious are the color, hardness, and shape of the seed pods. The dark brown capsules of the 28-chromosome species are hard and difficult to open and have rather blunt, rounded tips; in contrast, the lighter brown seed pods of the 40-chromosome species are more delicate. They are easily opened with the fingers and are more pointed at their tips, where a dried-up piece of the perianth tube that connected the flower with the ovary remains as a spike. These differences in shape are apparent when the capsule is nearing maturity but has not yet opened; after the tip of the capsule has opened, much of the defining shape is lost. See Plate 3 for a comparison of seed pods from two 28-chromosome species (*Iris sibirica* and *I. sanguinea*) and a 40-chromosome species (*I. forrestii*).

The other two morphological differences between the two groups are seen in the spathes and small flanges at the base of the falls. These are less obvious than the differences in the capsules. The spathes tend to be less than 2.5 inches (6 centimeters) long in the three species of subseries *Sibiricae* and 3 to 5 inches (7.5 to 12 centimeters) long in the species of subseries *Chrysographes*. The flanges are rather inconspicuous in both groups but are distinctly larger in the species of subseries *Chrysographes* (Figure 2-1; Plate 7).

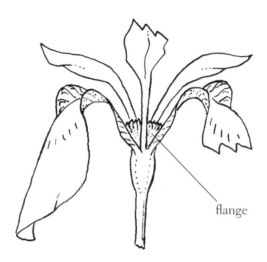

Figure 2-1. Flanges at the base of the falls of a 40-chromosome siberian iris.

On the basis of the similarities and differences between the two groups, Lee Lenz (1976) proposed a new classification of siberian irises leaving all the species in a single series but dividing series *Sibiricae* into two subseries: subseries *Sibiricae* for the species with twenty-eight chromosomes and subseries *Chrysographes* for those with forty. The differences between the two subseries are summarized in Table 2-1. Lenz's division of series *Sibiricae* into the two subseries has been adopted by the Society for Siberian Irises. Except for the addition of *Iris typhifolia*, news of which species first reached Europe and the United States in the late

Table 2-1. Differences between the two groups of siberian irises within series *Sibericae*.

	Subseries *Sibiricae*	Subseries *Chrysographes*
Species	I. sanguinea I. sibirica I. typhifolia	I. bulleyana I. chrysographes I. clarkei I. delavayi I. dykesii I. forrestii I. phragmitetorum[a] I. wilsonii
Geographic	Central Europe, northern Asia	Southwestern China
Cytogenetic	Chromosomes: $2n = 28$	Chromosomes: $2n = 40$
Morphologic		
Seed pods	Hard Dark brown Tips blunt	More delicate Lighter brown Tips spiked
Spathes	Short	Longer
Flanges	Small	Larger

[a] *Iris phragmitetorum*'s group is not certain.

1980s, and Lenz's subdivision of series *Sibiricae* into the two subseries, Lawrence's classification of the siberian irises remains unchanged.

Because the botanical names of the subseries are somewhat cumbersome in casual conversation, the Society for Siberian Irises's committee on nomenclature also looked at possible terms for common usage. Two in rather general currency at that time were "sino-siberians" for the 40-chromosome group and "garden siberians" for those with twenty-eight chromosomes, but those terms are inappropriate. Two of the three with twenty-eight chromosomes also come from China, and using the term "garden siberians" for the 28-chromosome group implies that the others are not suitable for the garden, which, of course, is not so. Furthermore, the term "garden siberians" is commonly and appropriately used for the modern cultivars to distinguish them from the wild species. Other, more geographically correct terms are "Eurasian group" for subseries *Sibiricae* and "South Asian group" for subseries *Chrysographes*. After considering these and other terms, the committee decided that the already widely employed terms "28-chromosome group" and "40-chromosome group" are most specific, and they became the chosen designations for informal use (McEwen 1977).

Although these terms were recommended, it must be borne in mind that tetraploids now exist, and since 1970, when the first tetraploid siberian irises were introduced, it has been necessary in classification to indicate whether a given cultivar is diploid or tetraploid. Tetraploids derived from plants of both subseries have twice the number of chromosomes found in the naturally occurring diploid plants and can therefore be referred to as either 28-chromosome group tetraploids or 40-chromosome group tetraploids. Hybrids between the two subseries can also occur, although very rarely; these presumably have a chromosome number of thirty-four. In short, the use of chromosome numbers as designations for the two groups presents a problem and raises the question of whether better names might not be selected as common garden terms.

Tetraploidy in Siberian Irises

Genes, the genetic determinants of every living thing, are contained in the cells in microscopic bodies called chromosomes. Every living organism has a characteristic number of chromosomes. Let us take the 28-

chromosome siberian irises as an example. In them, each somatic (body) cell has twenty-eight chromosomes, but the reproductive cells (inside the pollen grains and ovules) have half that number. At fertilization, each parent contributes fourteen chromosomes, and each somatic cell of the resulting seedling thus contains the characteristic number of twenty-eight. Since they involve two sets, one from each parent, these cells and the plants made up of them are called diploid, meaning "twofold." Through unknown causes, some plants, including several species of bearded irises, doubled their chromosomes in nature. Such plants have four sets of chromosomes and, hence, are called tetraploid (or "fourfold"). The tetraploid plants are superior to the diploid ones in certain respects, and botanists therefore sought means of inducing chromosome doubling, or tetraploidy, in the laboratory.

Many physical and chemical measures were attempted with little or no success until the 1930s, when it was discovered that doubling could be induced by colchicine, a drug derived from the autumn crocus, *Colchicum autumnale* (Eigsti and Dustin 1955). Although this use of colchicine was new, the drug itself is very old; crude extracts of colchicine were used as a medicine some 3000 years ago by the ancient Greeks. In modern times, colchicine has been used most often to treat acute attacks of gout.

Two terms that must be understood for this discussion are "polyploid" and "chimera." A polyploid is a plant with more than the normal diploid number of chromosomes, that is, chimeras, triploids, tetraploids, or those with still higher numbers of chromosomes. A chimera is a monster in Greek mythology, with the head of a lion, the body of a goat, and the tail of a serpent; hence the term was adopted by botanists to refer to a plant of mixed tissues, partly diploid and partly polyploid. Chimeras are of two general types: periclinal, in which all the flowers are partly diploid and partly polyploid, and sectorial, in which one section of the plant is diploid and the rest polyploid. Sectorial chimeras are interesting because they enable one to compare the diploid and polyploid form on the same plant. A sectorial siberian iris chimera is shown in Figure 2-2.

In the 1930s botanists began to use colchicine to induce tetraploidy in various grain crops, ornamental flowers, and other plants, but it was not tried with siberian irises until the 1960s. Max Steiger of Germany became the first to name a polyploid siberian iris, in 1964. This was 'Tetrafor', so named because it was derived from *Iris forrestii*. A first-generation induced polyploid, 'Tetrafor' was presumably only partly converted

Figure 2-2. A colchicine-induced sectorial chimera. On the left is a tetraploid flower and on the right a diploid flower of the same cultivar.

to the tetraploid state, and Steiger died before he could work with it further. Unfortunately, it and other plants in Steiger's garden were lost during his terminal illness.

My own interest in developing tetraploid siberian irises began in 1960 when the great hybridizer of tall bearded irises and daylilies, the late Orville Fay, showed me daylily seedlings he had treated with colchicine and explained his method of using the drug. As a rheumatologist, colchicine was very familiar to me. I had used it to treat hundreds of patients with acute gout, but I knew nothing of this newly discovered property. I was fascinated and started using Fay's method in 1961. In order to use colchicine in this new category of plants, I needed thousands of seeds, and my own siberian irises could not provide enough for a reasonable start. Fred Cassebeer kindly offered me "bee pod seeds" from his large collection of what were then the best-known named cultivars. This is why only the pod parent of my early tetraploids is known.

The first of my siberian irises successfully treated with colchicine bloomed in 1963, but since colchicine-induced (first-generation) tetraploids usually are only partly converted chimeras and can revert to the diploid state, I registered none until second-generation (and therefore fully tetraploid) seedlings were achieved. Thus it was not until 1970 that 'Orville Fay' and 'Fourfold White', the first tetraploid siberian irises to be registered and introduced, were named. Since then, many more have become available. Several hybridizers, including Robert M. Hollingworth in the United States and Tomas Tamberg and Eckard Berlin in Germany, have developed their own breeding lines using colchicine, and others are making good use of existing tetraploids in their hybridizing programs.

For a more detailed discussion of tetraploidy, including methods for inducing it and identification of resulting plants, see Appendix D.

Chapter 3

The Species

The eleven presumed species of siberian irises fall into two groups, subseries *Sibiricae* with twenty-eight somatic chromosomes and subseries *Chrysographes* with forty. In this chapter each species is described in general garden terms, with particular reference to the features that distinguish it from the others. Those of which authentic living specimens exist are illustrated in the watercolors by Jean Witt (Plates 1 through 9). Species of the two groups are discussed separately. In each group they are taken up in the order of their discovery.

Subseries *Sibiricae*

Iris sibirica

Iris sibirica (Plate 1) is the species that has given its name to the entire series and subseries. The stalks are 30 to 48 inches (75 to 120 centimeters) tall and carry their flowers some 6 inches (15 centimeters) or more above the leaves. Leaves are 0.25 to 0.5 inch (6 to 12 millimeters) wide. The stalks have one to three branches carrying multiple buds. There may be up to five buds at the terminal (but three is more usual) and two more at each branch. The spathes are dry and already turning brown by flowering time, and the individual pedicels are very unequal in length. The flowers are 2.5 to 3 inches (6 to 7.5 centimeters) in diameter and have rather narrow, arching, pendent falls approximately 0.75 inch (2 centimeters) wide. The slender standards are very upright and are blue-violet in color. The falls have a base color of white overlaid with blue-violet veins, which become so merged at the outer half of the falls that the white is obscured. The capsules are less than twice as long as wide (Plate 3). *Iris sibirica* is the only species of siberian iris whose natural range lies outside Asia. It is found in western and southern Europe, northwestern Turkey, and southern Russia, as far east as Lake Baikal (Rodionenko 1964, 1992). One alleged specimen of *I. sibirica* is reported to have been collected by Francis Kingdon-Ward in Tibet (Waddick 1993).

The flowers are usually as described, but those of individual plants can be quite different. In 1974 I had the opportunity to see thousands of plants of *Iris sibirica* growing in the wild in a somewhat boggy field near the town of Langenargen, close to the Bodensee (Lake Constance) in Germany. The majority fit the species profile, but in about a quarter of the population the standards were reddish blue rather than violet-blue. In another quarter or so the white markings between the colored veins were very pronounced, and in perhaps 5 percent the falls were entirely white except for fine blue veins extending out to the tips. In a small number—perhaps 1 percent—the falls were nearly horizontal instead of being pendent. Many had two or three branches (McEwen 1974a). Variations of this sort undoubtedly occur in large natural populations of other species of both subseries.

Iris sanguinea

The stalks of *Iris sanguinea* (Plate 2) are approximately the same height as the leaves. Leaves are 0.25 to 0.5 inch (6 to 12 millimeters) wide. *Iris sanguinea* has no branches and only two buds. The spathes are green and fresh at time of flowering and often are suffused with pink or red at their bases. The flowers are larger than those of *I. sibirica*, and the falls wider and rounder. Pedicels are about equal in length and 1 to 2 inches (2.5 to 5 centimeters) long. The capsules are three times as long as wide (Plate 3). The flower color is similar to that of *I. sibirica*, but the white areas between the violet-blue veins are more distinct and the outer half of the falls is entirely violet-blue. The geographic distribution includes western and eastern Siberia, Korea, northeast China, and Japan.

Iris typhifolia

Iris typhifolia (Plate 4), the most recently discovered species, was found in China in 1928 and described soon after (Kitagawa 1939) but was not known in the West until 1988. The plant is similar to *I. sibirica* except that the leaves are very slender, only 0.10 to 0.25 inch (3 to 6 millimeters) wide. The flower also resembles that of *I. sibirica*, but the falls are more arching and the color is rich, dark bluish purple, with only slight evidence of white at the signal areas. The pedicels are of markedly unequal length at bloom time. Some plants from collected seeds have no branches, but others have one or two. Its season of bloom is very early. Seed pods, typical of a 28-chromosome species, have rather blunt tips and are more than three times as long as wide. Although the chromosomes of *I. typhifolia* have not been counted, there has been no hesitation in placing it in the 28-chromosome group because of its appearance, the character of its capsules, and the readiness with which it crosses with other 28-chromosome siberian irises. Its range is limited to extreme northeast China, in Nei Menggu (Inner Mongolia), Jilin, and Liaoning Provinces.

Subseries *Chrysographes*

Iris clarkei

Iris clarkei (Plate 5) differs from all other siberian iris species in having solid stalks. Leaves are shorter than stalks, which are approximately 24 inches (60 centimeters) tall and have one to three branches. The standards are held almost horizontally and are somewhat reddish purple. The arched, pendent falls are violet-blue to reddish blue, with prominent white patches at the signal areas. This species grows along streams in damp sites near lakes in eastern Nepal, Sikkim, Bhutan, northeast India, upper Burma, Yunnan Province in China, and southern Tibet.

Iris delavayi

The leaves of *Iris delavayi* (Plate 6) are distinctly shorter than the stalks, which usually reach 3 to 4 feet (90 to 120 centimeters) but can be as tall as 5 feet (150 centimeters). There may be one to three branches with up to two buds each. Standards are fairly upright and the falls arched and pendent. The color is rich purple, with white markings at the signal areas. This species grows in wet meadow areas in southwest Sichuan and northern Yunnan Provinces in China.

Iris wilsonii and Iris forrestii

The two yellow species, *Iris wilsonii* (Plate 7) and *I. forrestii* (Plate 8), can be considered together. The flowers of *I. wilsonii* are somewhat larger than those of *I. forrestii* and their color somewhat lighter. The falls of both are marked slightly by reddish brown veins and dots, which are more prominent in *I. wilsonii*. Neither species is branched. The most distinguishing features are the standards and pedicels. In *I. forrestii*, the standards are upright, but they are held at 50 degrees or more from upright in *I. wilsonii*. And whereas the pedicels are short in *I. forrestii*, they are 3 to 4 inches (7.5 to 10 centimeters) long in *I. wilsonii*. Stalks of *I. forrestii* are somewhat taller than the leaves; in *I. wilsonii*, leaves and stalks are about equal in length. In general *I. wilsonii* makes a more robust clump than *I. forrestii* and blooms several weeks later. Seed pods of both *I. wilsonii* and *I. forrestii* are typical of 40-chromosome species (Plate 3). The distribution of *I. forrestii* is limited to open meadows at 12,000 to 13,000 feet (3660 to 3900 meters) on the eastern flank of the Lichiang Range in northwestern Yunnan, Sichuan, and Tibet Provinces in China and in adjacent Burma. *Iris wilsonii* also grows in high alpine meadows, but over a wider area, encompassing Hubei, Shaanxi, Gansu, southwest Sichuan, and mid-Yunnan Provinces.

Iris chrysographes

Iris chrysographes (Plate 9), which gives its name to the subseries, is the darkest in color of the species, a rich reddish purple that in some cultivars approaches black. The dark falls are set off in most plants by a few golden lines at the base of the falls, from which markings the species gets its name of "golden writing." Some natural examples of the species occur in somewhat pink tones. The leaves are approximately 20 inches (50 centimeters) tall as are also the unbranched stalks. The natural habitat of this species includes southern Sichuan and western Yunnan Provinces in China and upper Burma, where it is found growing at 4000 to 11,000 feet (1220 to 3350 meters).

Iris bulleyana

Iris bulleyana has been a subject of much uncertainty almost from the time of its naming by Dykes in 1910. Arthur K. Bulley raised the original plants, which Dykes believed had come from seeds sent by George Forrest, who was collecting in China for Bulley. Forrest could not later recall having seen any plants resembling *I. bulleyana* growing in the wild, however, nor did his field notes contain any helpful information (Grey-Wilson 1971; Davidson 1982). Nevertheless, John Macqueen Cowan (1952) states that Forrest brought back herbarium specimens from southeast Tibet and Yunnan that are identical with the plant that Dykes tended in his garden, received from and named for Bulley (Witt 1971a).

Zhao Yu-tang has reported the wide distribution of a species he calls *Iris bulleyana* growing at 2300 to 3500 feet (700 to 1070 meters) in Sichuan, Yunnan, and Tibet Provinces in southwest China. He describes the plant thus: leaves 20 inches (50 centimeters) long and 0.05 to 0.25 inch (1.5 to 6 millimeters) wide; leaves and stalks approximately equal in height; no branch and two buds; blue-purple standards 30 degrees from upright; and mottled blue-purple falls, semi-flaring. These plants are reported to be different from the *I. bulleyana* named by Dykes (Waddick 1993). In 1980 Zhao described *I. bulleyana* f. *alba*, a form with creamy white flowers native to Yunnan Province, where it is found growing in hillside meadows and beside streams (Waddick and Zhao 1992).

Davidson (1974), who has seen the collection at the herbarium of the Royal Botanic Gardens, Kew, in England, comments on three sheets of material there identified as *Iris bulleyana*. Two specimens—one collected in 1893 by Jean André Soulié in eastern Tibet and another by O. Schloch in 1916 in Yunnan—are rather robust plants, but a third, attributed to Henry McLaren's collectors in western China in 1933, is a very small, slender plant, only half the size of the other two. McLaren's native collectors were the same as those Forrest had employed.

Eleven years after his description of *Iris bulleyana*, Dykes had second thoughts about the iris he named. He wrote in the 23 June 1921 issue of *The Garden* that "*bulleyana* seems to be of hybrid origin as it does not breed true from seed. Its parents, however, are unknown and there is no suggestion as to which species could have given rise to it." He mentioned also that "it grows to about two feet with somewhat narrow leaves and flowers veined and blotched on a white ground" (Davidson 1982). The painting by Frank Harold Round in Dykes's *The Genus Iris* depicts a mottled flower of semi-flaring form with no branch and with capsules typical of the 40-chromosome group of siberian irises.

It has been suggested that Dykes's plant originated not from seed carried back from China but in Bulley's garden, as a natural hybrid of *Iris chrysographes* and *I. forrestii* or *I. wilsonii*. If that parentage is correct, however, the natural cross must have occurred in China since *I. wilsonii* was collected in 1907 and *I. forrestii* and *I. chrysographes* in 1908, and there would not have been time for them to produce a seedling in England that would have bloomed by 1910. That such a cross could have occurred in China is certainly possible.

Clearly the status of *Iris bulleyana* remains uncertain. The statement by Zhao (Waddick and Zhao 1992) that it is found in China would appear to indicate that such a species, or at least such a plant, exists, but there can be no doubt that the cultivar grown by Dykes was a hybrid (Hansford 1968; McEwen 1971a; Davidson 1982). To add to the confusion, plants that actually were *I. sibirica* were mislabeled and distributed for several years as *I. bulleyana* (Davidson 1982).

The story of *Iris bulleyana* serves well to illustrate the problems involved in identification of species and the need for further botanical collecting, not only to search for new species but also to reappraise those already known.

Iris dykesii

The status of *Iris dykesii* as a species is even more doubtful than that of *I. bulleyana*. It is said to have come to Dykes from St. Petersburg, Russia, although Dykes himself thought it originated in western China. He believed the plant might be a new species, but he never saw the flower, which did not bloom until after his death. A neighbor, Charles Musgrave, moved it to his own garden, where it first bloomed in 1926. The specimen plant as grown by Musgrave is illustrated in color in *Curtis's Botanical Magazine* (1933, volume 155, plate 9282), showing a plant with leaves equal in height to the unbranched stalks. The leaves are relatively wide (0.75 inch, or 2 centimeters) and enfold the stalks for the greater part of their length. The flowers somewhat resemble those of *I. chrysographes*, but they are larger, with wider falls. The color is brilliant dark violet-purple, with yellow and white lines at the base of the falls. It appears to be unknown in China, as it is not listed in Zhao's contribution to *Iris of China* (Waddick and Zhao

1992). On the basis of current information, it seems very improbable that it is a true species.

Iris phragmitetorum

The species of the 28- and 40-chromosome groups have been discussed thus far in the order of their discovery. The exception is *Iris phragmitetorum*, which has been held until last because it is not certain to which of the two groups it belongs.

Iris phragmitetorum was collected by Heinrich Handel-Mazzetti in 1916, in a reedy (*Phragmites*) swamp near what is now Kunming City, the capital of Yunnan Province, China. It exists only as an herbarium specimen at the Royal Botanic Gardens, Kew, and has never been known in the living state outside of China. Indeed, the swamp in which Handel-Mazzetti discovered *I. phragmitetorum* has disappeared with the growth of Kunming City, and it has long been feared that this species no longer exists. The *Register of Seed Plants of Yunnan* (1987, page 878) lists it as "found at altitudes of 1890–3200 meters in the marshland near the lake, Dian Chi Kunming, Dali." Sheng Jue-min reports seeing a potted specimen blooming in July 1987 at a small inn at the lakeside resort village of Dian Chi, a few kilometers south of Kunming City; the flowers were described as being an attractive blue color (Waddick 1992). Although these more recent notes give hope that new examples of it may yet be uncovered, Waddick found no trace of it in his collecting visit to China in 1993.

Because its chromosome number has never been ascertained and the herbarium specimen at the Royal Botanic Gardens, Kew, does not include such features as seed pods, which might permit a decision, it is not certain to which group *Iris phragmitetorum* belongs. Its discovery in Yunnan points to the 40-chromosome group. The specimen at Kew is thought to have similarities to both *I. sanguinea* and a specimen identified as *I. chrysographes* (Davidson 1992). A note in C. H. Grey's *Hardy Bulbs* (1938) states that Handel-Mazzetti considered it "clearly akin to *I. clarkei*" (Davidson 1977). In view of the opinion expressed by its discoverer, the weight of evidence favors its being a member of the 40-chromosome group.

In closing this discussion of the individual species, I must point out the uncertainty of some of our assumptions regarding the species, especially those of subseries *Chrysographes*. The serious questions concerning *Iris bulleyana, I. dykesii,* and *I. phragmitetorum* have been detailed. In addition, in view of the inaccessibility of many areas where the species grow, the many years that have elapsed since the early collections, and the possibility of natural hybridization, one must admit at least some degree of uncertainty about many specimens of the presumed species grown in the United States and other countries today. Continued study of these and indeed all the irises in China and other Asian countries remains a pressing need.

Chapter 4

Characteristics
of
Modern Cultivars

The features that characterize the eleven species have been discussed in Chapter 3. This chapter is concerned with the characteristics of the modern cultivated siberian irises, considered separately for cultivars of the 28-chromosome group (subseries *Sibiricae*), those of the 40-chromosome group (subseries *Chrysographes*), and tetraploids. First, however, it will be useful to review briefly the anatomical features of the siberian iris flower as illustrated in Figure 4-1, which shows a flower with certain portions removed and manipulated so that others may be seen. In their natural arrangement, the styles cover the anthers, and the spathes enclose the ovary. The detached style is shown in an upright position to reveal the stigma on its undersurface.

Subseries *Sibiricae*

Size

Specific, precisely defined categories of size have not been established for siberian irises as they have been for the bearded irises, but various cultivars differ considerably in this respect all the same (Plate 11). Most modern siberian irises have flowers 3 to 4 inches (7.5 to 10 centimeters) in diameter carried on stalks 2 to 4 feet (60 to 120 centimeters) tall, but there are exceptions to the rule. Many are larger and taller; oth-

25

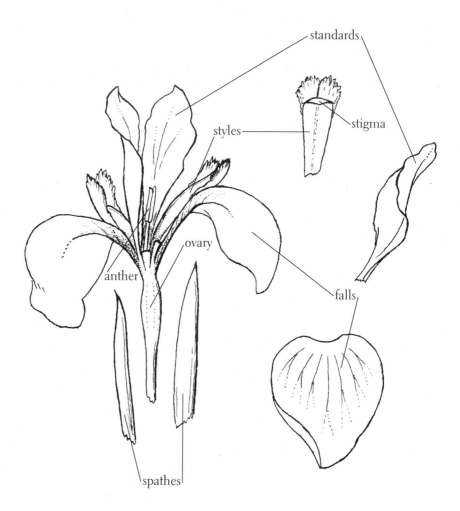

Figure 4-1. The anatomical features of the siberian iris flower.

ers, usually referred to as miniatures, or dwarfs, have smaller flowers on shorter stalks. The largest diploid flowers approach 5 inches (12 centimeters) in diameter, and some tetraploids reach 6 inches (15 centimeters). A miniature, *Iris sibirica* 'Acuta', was named as early as 1813, and Amos Perry listed two in 1940, 'Nana' with lavender flowers and 'Nana Alba', a lovely white miniature. It should be noted that its characteristics strongly suggest that 'Nana Alba' is a miniature form of *I. sanguinea* rather than of *I. sibirica* (McEwen 1978b; Witt 1992). Since the 1970s interest in breeding miniatures has grown; several results of this hybridizing effort are less than 18 inches (45 centimeters) tall and a few, such as 'Baby Sister' and 'Precious Doll', are still smaller, with 2.5-inch (6-centimeter) flowers carried on stalks less than 10 inches (25 centimeters) tall. Most miniature siberian irises tend to grow a few inches taller after three or four years, but if then divided and replanted, they return to their original diminutive height.

Rhizomes and roots

Rhizomes of siberian irises are so much smaller than those of tall bearded irises that growers familiar with the bearded cultivars may actually have trouble recognizing them. The more slender roots of siberians also differ from the thicker roots of their bearded cousins.

Leaves and stalks

The overall appearance of the plant is one of the excellent features of siberian irises. The leaves are held fully erect or gracefully arching in their upper thirds, and the stalks are likewise upright and elegant (Plates 11 and 12). Some older cultivars and seedlings have leaves that tend to fall over and sprawl as the season advances; such plants no longer deserve a place in the garden. Another excellent feature of the leaves is the green color they maintain all through the summer. By late fall, some browning may occur at the tips of leaves, but even then the plants are rarely unattractive. Siberian irises are remarkably healthy, vigorous plants and, with very rare exceptions, are not subject to the spotting and streaking of the leaves seen in some other irises. The attractive architectural value of the foliage, even when the flowers are not in bloom, is a major advantage in the garden.

The bloom stalks may hold their flowers 1 foot (30 centimeters) or more above the leaves, or the flowers may float charmingly just above the leaves. Not surprisingly, flowers that are lost in the leaves by being held too low are very undesirable. There may be no branch or one or two branches in addition to the terminal; rarely, as many as three branches occur. Two or three buds are commonly held at the terminal and one or two on each branch. The height of the stalks and the amount of branching reflect the relative influence of *Iris sibirica* and *I. sanguinea* in the genetic background of the particular cultivar.

Form

What may be thought of as the traditional form of siberian irises is that of the species (Plates 1 through 10) and of seedlings derived directly from them or from crossing them. The characteristic feature of these flowers is the pendent position of the relatively narrow falls (Figure 4-2).

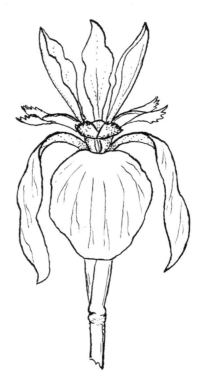

Figure 4-2. The pendent falls of *Iris sibirica*.

With selective breeding and increasing use of *Iris sanguinea*, falls gradually became more arching and wider (Figure 4-3), and since the advent of 'White Swirl' (Plate 12) many falls are flaring or semi-flaring and round (Figure 4-4).

Falls and standards may be rather tailored (Plate 13) or ruffled (Plates 14 and 26) and the edges smooth (Plate 13) or crimped (Plates 14 and 24). Among flowers with flaring falls, some have rather

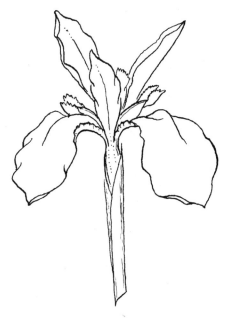

Figure 4-3. The arched falls of 'White Magnificence'.

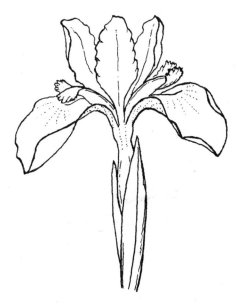

Figure 4-4. A flower with semi-flaring falls.

open form with spaces between the falls (Figure 4-5). Others with open form are lent a different appearance by their larger, rounder falls (Plates 13 and 27). In others, the standards tend to fill the open spaces (Figure 4-6; Plates 17 and 18), giving them a quite round appearance, and some even have overlapping falls (Figure 4-7; Plate 26). The Society for Siberian Irises considers all these forms desirable. In the garden, a contrast of forms heightens the beauty and interest of the planting.

Figure 4-5. A flower with flaring falls and open form.

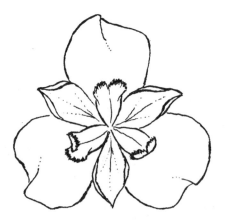

Figure 4-6. The standards of 'White Swirl' partly fill the spaces between the wider, rounder falls, giving a rounder form to the flower.

Figure 4-7. The very wide, overlapping falls of this flower create a very round form.

Two new forms of siberian irises have been developed by Ho Shidara in Japan. One is similar to the double japanese iris, with six falls and no standards (Plate 15). The other is multipetalled, with extra petals at the center in addition to the six falls (Plate 16).

Since the 1980s, flowers with unusually wide and attractive styles have appeared, particularly in tetraploid cultivars. The styles of most siberian irises are approximately 0.75 inch (2 centimeters) wide, but many cultivars now have styles 1 inch (2.5 centimeters) wide, and some measure as much as 2 inches (5 centimeters) across. In addition, these wide styles usually are topped by large, tufted crests, and many have marked feathering, or fimbriation, of the midribs. Such styles add a most attractive new dimension to the flowers (Plates 17, 20, and 24).

Color

The predominant color of flowers of the 28-chromosome group is blue, in shades ranging from light violet-blue (Plate 13) to dark bluish purple (Plates 18 and 26). True blue as depicted in the Royal Horticultural Society's color charts was slow in coming but has been achieved. The other color present in the 28-chromosome species is white, and many lovely flowers of pure white (Plate 19) and creamy white (Plate 20) have been realized. Although some give the impression of immaculate whiteness, a suffusion of yellow is found at the base of the falls in most. No flowers of spectrum red or true pink exist, but here again hybridizers are making some progress (see 'Windwood Serenade' on the cover, and Plates 21 and 22). Whereas two yellow species occur in the 40-chromosome group, yellow did not exist in the 28-chromosome siberian irises until the 1970s, when 'Butter and Sugar' appeared (Plate 23). Since then many more cultivars with yellow falls and white standards have been introduced, and flowers with even richer yellow falls and some yellow in the standards are also available (Plate 24).

Signals and patterns

In blue, red, and pink flowers, a striking feature appears in the same place as the suffusion of yellow in white flowers, at the base of the falls. It is a semicircular design known as the signal, or blaze. In many of the older siberian irises the signals were tinged with unattractive brownish yellow markings, but most modern cultivars have white (Plate 13) or gold (Plate 27) signals that add much to the beauty of the flower. Signals differ greatly in their impact from flower to flower. In most cultivars they are rather unobtrusive (Plate 13), in others they are a major feature (Plate 18), and in others they tend to be covered by the styles and are scarcely seen (Plate 26). All such variations are desirable and add interest to the individual flower and to the planting as a whole.

In addition to the signals, many flowers have other patterns that enhance their unique beauty. These include a wire-thin white or gold edging around dark falls (Plate 27); stippled or dappled patterns on falls (Plate 28); and contrasting colors of falls, standards, and styles, in bitones (Plate 29) and bicolors (Plate 30). In some flowers, warm yellow or cool green veins spread down from the signals over the falls, a most attractive feature. Green veins radiating from greenish signals give an especially fresh, appealing appearance to white flowers. A new pattern—white lines and dots splashed over blue falls—appeared in 1994 (Plate 25).

Texture

Texture may be defined as the surface character of the petals, whether it be glossy, matte, or velvety. Velvety texture gives a particularly rich color to red and purple flowers (Plate 18). Some falls of glossy texture glint as though diamond-dusted.

Substance

Substance refers to the deep-tissue quality of the petals and encompasses such characteristics as thickness and flexibility. What constitutes desirable substance depends on the form of the flower. All flowers with pendent falls and most with lightly arched falls should have flexible substance, which allows them to flutter attractively. On the other hand, flowers of flaring form need firmer substance. A flower with marked firmness of substance is often referred to as starchy or leathery.

Durability

Durability has sometimes been confused with substance but is entirely different. It refers to the capacity of the flower to remain handsome for the normal number of days and to withstand adverse stresses, such as wind, rain, and hot weather. Flowers of flexible, more delicate substance can be just as durable as those of firm substance. Siberian iris flowers remain handsome for two to four days depending largely on the local temperature and humidity. The flowers of most cultivars then dry up and become unobtrusive or fall off within a week, and thus they are not long unattractive, even if left on the plant.

Time and length of bloom

Date of bloom depends upon climatic conditions, of course, and will differ greatly from southern to northern regions, in both hemispheres. In general, the earliest members of the 28-chromosome group start to bloom a week or so before peak bloom of the tall bearded irises, with a peak bloom approximately a week after that of the tall beardeds. Cultivars with no branch and only two buds can be expected to bloom no longer than ten days unless they have the capacity to send up successive bloom stalks. The average cultivar with one or two branches may bloom for three weeks. By selecting cultivars that bloom early, mid-season, and late, the gardener can enjoy a bloom period of six weeks or more.

The bloom period is extended still longer by plants that have the valuable trait of being able to flower a second time. This second period of bloom differs strikingly from rebloom in bearded irises. In siberian irises, it comes after a relatively brief "rest period" of one to several weeks, whereas the bearded irises rebloom only after an interval of several months. To emphasize the difference from rebloom of bearded irises, the early second bloom in the siberians (and japanese) irises is referred to as repeat bloom (Plate 31).

On the basis of their behavior with regard to repeat bloom, siberian and japanese irises have been divided into four categories: 1) the great number that lack the capacity; 2) the occasional repeaters, which sometimes bloom a second time; 3) the reliable repeaters, which can be expected to repeat each year if growing well; and 4) the preferential repeaters, which bloom better the second time than the first. A separate category is that of continuing bloomers. In the repeaters, no new bloom stalks are apparent for a few days after the end of first bloom. In the continuing bloomers, new bloom stalks continue to appear without pause until the final end of bloom (McEwen 1983).

The ability to repeat is a genetic trait, as my own experience well demonstrates. I crossed two seedlings that repeated excellently, resulting in roughly 50 percent repeaters. Crossing the best of these gave more than 80 percent repeaters, many of them preferential (McEwen 1979). Repeat bloom nevertheless demands good culture in addition to genetic predisposition. A seedling that lacks the genetic determinant to repeat will have no second period of bloom even if growing perfectly. On the other hand, a seedling with the genetic trait may not repeat if growing poorly. Ample water and an application of fertilizer, preferably soluble, shortly before and after first bloom help to bring out the trait.

Repeat bloomers have been available at least since 1949, when Elizabeth Scheffy introduced 'My Love', and Marjorie Brummitt obviously recognized that particular feature when she named her 'Violet Repeat' in 1967. A few, such as Jean Witt's 'Echo Two', a 40-chromosome repeater, can also rebloom in the fall, but this is very unusual.

Fragrance

One of the charms of tall bearded irises is their lovely fragrance, but unfortunately, siberian irises have lacked this attribute. Only since 1985, with the introduction of 'Mabel Coday', has a fragrant cultivar been available, and in it the fragrance is so delicate that not everyone can appreciate it. This is a trait that clearly warrants greater effort by hybridizers.

Subseries *Chrysographes*

In general the characteristics of the modern cultivars of 40-chromosome siberian irises are similar to those of the 28-chromosome group and therefore can be discussed more briefly.

Size

Flowers tend to be somewhat smaller than those of the 28-chromosome group. The height of the stalks is 1 to 5 feet (30 to 150 centimeters), depending largely on which of the particular species have been used as parents. I know of no miniatures.

Leaves and stalks

Leaves are narrower and more arching than those of the 28-chromosome group. Stalks are similar except that many of them have no branches and only two buds, depending on which species made up the cross. Only *Iris clarkei* and *I. delavayi* of the 40-chromosome species have branches. Selective breeding using these species and their seedlings has led to some modern cultivars with one to three branches and up to eight buds.

Form

The flowers of earlier cultivars are all of pendent or arching form, but through selective breeding the semi-flaring form has been obtained in modern cultivars (McGarvey 1975).

Color

As would be expected, color depends on the parents. Seedlings from crosses of *Iris forrestii* with *I. wilsonii* are, of course, yellow or cream colored (Plate 32). Crossing the violet-blue and purple species has resulted in many seedlings in those colors, often with unusual patterns (Plate 33). Many interesting dotted and striped seedlings have been achieved by crossing *I. chrysographes* and other dark parents with yellow parents.

Time of bloom

The 40-chromosome species and seedlings from them tend to bloom a week or more after peak bloom of the 28-chromosome group and, hence, are useful in extending the season of bloom.

Tetraploid Siberian Irises

Tetraploid siberian irises derived from the 28-chromosome group share the characteristics of their diploid relatives but with a few differences. The flowers are larger, some reaching 6 inches (15 centimeters) in diameter (Figure 2-2), and the leaves and stalks are stouter but not taller. The leaves are darker green, and the colors of the flowers are richer; the pigments are the same as those in the diploid flowers, but each cell contains roughly twice as much and therefore the concentration of color is greater. Such desirable features as ruffling, velvety texture, and wide, tufted styles tend to be more pronounced. Against these advantages there are some faults. Stouter stalks and stiffer flowers can result in some loss of grace, and occasionally stalks can be too short, so that the flowers are lost in the leaves.

Color
Plates

Plate 1. *Iris sibirica*.

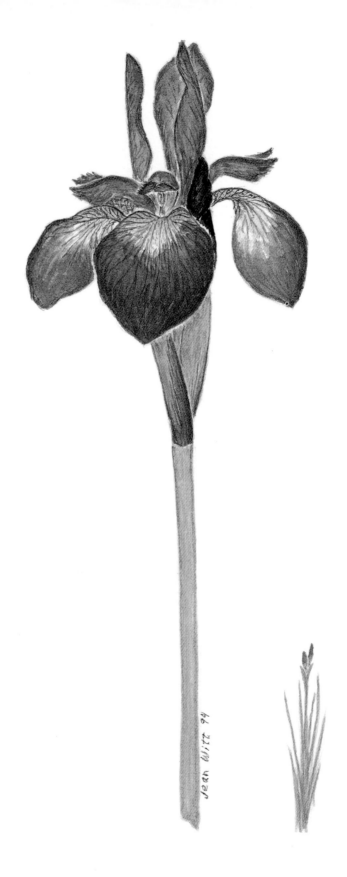

Plate 2. *Iris sanguinea.*

Plate 3. Seed pods of (left to right) *Iris sibirica*, *I. sanguinea*, and *I. forrestii*.

Plate 4. *Iris typhifolia*.

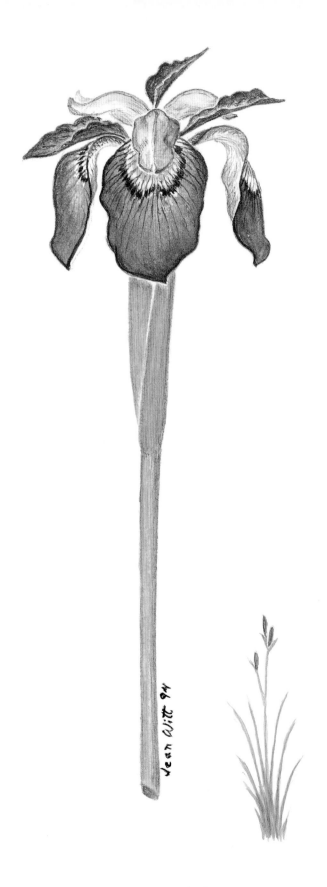

Plate 5. *Iris clarkei*.

Plate 6. *Iris delavayi.*

Plate 7. *Iris wilsonii*.

Plate 8. *Iris forrestii*.

Plate 9. *Iris chrysographes*.

Plate 10. *Iris sanguinea* growing wild in the foothills of Mount Fuji, near Asagiri, Japan.

Plate 11. Siberian irises in a range of different sizes and heights. 'Nana Alba' is on the left, 'Ego' and 'Anniversary' on the right, with other taller cultivars behind.

Plate 12. 'White Swirl', Fred Cassebeer's milestone in the development of the modern siberian irises.

Plate 13. 'Lady of Quality', a tetraploid with tailored, open form; smooth edges; unobtrusive white signals of usual size; and slight silver edging.

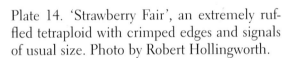

Plate 14. 'Strawberry Fair', an extremely ruffled tetraploid with crimped edges and signals of usual size. Photo by Robert Hollingworth.

Plate 15. 'Nagarakashi', a diploid with six falls. Photo by Robert Hollingworth.

Plate 16. 'Raman', a multipetalled diploid. Photo by Robert Hollingworth.

Plate 17. 'Harpswell Love', a large tetraploid whose tufted styles are as wide as its standards. The yellow at the base of each fall is characteristic of white siberian irises.

Plate 18. 'Shirley Pope', a diploid with large white signals and a velvety texture: note the effect on the tips of the upper and lower right falls.

Plate 19. 'White Triangles', a pure white diploid of triangular form. Photo by Edward White.

Plate 20. 'Harpswell Moonlight', a creamy white tetraploid with wide, tufted styles.

Plate 21. 'Hubbard', a wine-red tetraploid with green in throat.

Plate 22. 'Pink Haze', introduced in 1969 and still the standard of comparison for newer pinks. Photo by Elsie McGarvey.

Plate 23. 'Butter and Sugar', the first nonfading yellow amoena diploid. Photo by Chandler Fulton.

Plate 24. 'Butter and Cream', a tetraploid descended from 'Butter and Sugar' with a central cup formed by position of standards and styles. Note the richer yellow falls; the increased yellow of the standards; the darker, crimped edges; and the fimbriation of style midribs.

Plate 25. 'Neat Trick', a diploid, whose signals burst over the blue falls with dots and streaks of white. Photo by Edward White.

Plate 26. 'Ruffled Round', a large dark tetraploid with wide, ruffled, overlapping falls and an absence of obvious signals.

Plate 27. 'Golden Edge', a tetraploid with gold signals, edged pattern, and open form.

Plate 28. 'Ann Dasch', a diploid with a dappled pattern. Photo by Steve Varner.

Plate 29. 'Springs Brook', a bitoned diploid. Photo by Martin Schafer.

Plate 30. 'Rill', a bicolored diploid. Photo by Don Herres.

Plate 31. 'Welcome Return', a tetraploid repeater, showing large pods from first bloom period and a new flower on a repeating stalk.

Plate 32. 'Cascade Creme', a lovely cream-colored diploid of the 40-chromosome group. Photo by Lorena Reid.

Plate 33. 'Dotted Line', a 40-chromosome cultivar from blue breeding. Photo by Lorena Reid.

Plate 34. 'Golden Waves', a diploid Calsibe from yellow breeding. Photo by Lorena Reid.

Plate 35. An unnamed tetraploid Calsibe seedling of Tomas Tamberg. Photo by Tomas Tamberg.

Plate 36. A mass planting of siberian irises at Windwood Gardens, Williamston, Michigan. Photo by Robert Hollingworth.

Plate 37. 'Limeheart', featured in Roger R. Nelson's garden in Brooks, Oregon. Photo by Robert Hollingworth.

Chapter 5

Culture

This chapter is concerned with the planting and care of mature plants, with various aspects of siberian iris culture considered primarily for the 28-chromosome group; the particular cultural needs of the 40-chromosome cultivars and potted siberian irises are then discussed more briefly, along with recommendations for shipping plants. The handling of seeds and seedlings is treated in Chapter 10.

Subseries *Sibiricae*

Siberian irises of the 28-chromosome group are among the easiest, least demanding perennials to grow. They can be naturalized in a field and given essentially no care, and still they bloom year after year, provided merely that their leaves are not mowed until they turn brown in the fall. Certainly such plants do not flourish and bloom is meager, but they survive. My purpose in this chapter is rather to discuss the conditions under which these irises thrive.

Climate

The 28-chromosome siberian irises are adaptable to a wide range of climatic conditions. They are extremely cold hardy (Rodionenko 1992). Both *Iris sanguinea*, native to Siberia, and *I. sibirica* withstand severe cold, hence it is not surprising that the modern hybrids derived from these species share their hardiness. And since 1988 *I. typhifolia* too has been used in the West as a hybridizing parent. Since it is native to China's northernmost provinces, there can be no doubt that the seedlings resulting from crosses involving it, *I. sibirica*, and *I. sanguinea* will inherit high cold tolerance. The modern 28-chromosome hybrids flourish in all temperate regions with ample annual rainfall but are less at home in the deep south. In hot, arid regions they are far more difficult to grow and require special measures, such as shade, mulch, and extra water.

Site selection

Except in hot, arid areas, these irises like full sun. They will bloom quite well with a minimum of a half day of sun, but with less than that have scant bloom and gradually deteriorate. They tolerate a wide range of soils but are not at their best under alkaline conditions.

Although siberian irises resist wind damage as well as most perennials, large, open garden areas in places with high winds will profit from some protection. In our large hybridizing beds on the coast of Maine, we left a screen of wild rugosa roses and other native bushes when the garden was bulldozed out of the original overgrown site. Such a screen should be at least 6 feet (1.8 meters) from the cultivated area to prevent invasion by roots.

Choose a site that has adequate soil drainage. Siberian irises relish abundant water, and in fact will stand flooding for short periods very well (Stark 1974), but they cannot endure standing water during their dormant period. They are particularly at home planted at the edge of a natural pond or along a brook, where their roots can be constantly moist, so long as their crowns are well above water level. Such poolside plantings may be disadvantageous, however, if the pool contains fish or frogs; in the event some future infestation requires pesticidal sprays, the animals might be harmed by the runoff of toxic substances.

Preparing a new bed

Many readers no doubt have garden beds available for planting; this section is intended for those who must create a new bed from scratch. If the site is in an area of bushes and grass, start preparing the bed at least three months before the desired planting time. Begin by removing all large stones and unwanted bushes and their roots. Follow this with an application of a nonselective herbicide, such as glyphosate (see Table 5-2), to kill grass and weeds; do this on a windless day and with great care, to prevent damage to any desirable plants nearby. Thoroughly dig or till the soil, then spread and till in manure. Partly composted manure can be used if planting is scheduled for the following spring, but if planting is to be done shortly after the new bed is finished, only thoroughly composted (approximately three years old) manure is suitable.

Depending on the nature of the soil, varying amounts of other materials may be added. Compost and peat moss are best and improve both sandy soils and soils with too much clay. For exceedingly clayey soils, sand as well as the organic materials may be worked in, but the addition of compost, peat moss, and other organic materials is usually sufficient.

It is a good idea to test the chemical reaction of the soil during this preparatory stage, to determine whether it is acidic, neutral, or alkaline. Simple kits are available at garden stores; more complete tests can be done by the local University Cooperative Extension Service or other laboratories. The unit of measurement is known as the pH (hydrogen ion concentration). A pH of 7 is neutral. Any numbers above that indicate increasingly greater alkalinity; numbers below 7 indicate increasingly greater acidity. Siberian irises tolerate such a wide pH range that rarely is there need for correction of the soil's reaction. If the pH is 7.8 or higher, however, it should be lowered, which is easily done. Scatter agricultural sulfur over the bed at the rate of 1.5 pounds (680 grams) per 100 square feet (8 square meters) and till it in deeply. This reduces the pH by roughly three quarters of a point. The amount applied can, of course, be adjusted depending on the initial pH and the level desired. With passing time the pH will gradually return to that of the surrounding untreated soil. If the water of the region also has an alkaline pH, as it often does where soil is naturally alkaline, repeat the agricultural sulfur treatment every few years as indicated by annual tests of the soil pH. Agricultural sulfur requires approximately six months to achieve its full effect, so the sooner the treatment can be done, the better.

Finally, do not be discouraged if these adjustments of the physical condition of the soil and its reactivity sound too difficult. The removal of rocks, grass, and bushes, good digging or tilling, and the incorporation of composted manure and other organic material are all that is needed to prepare the bed in all but the rarest situations.

Time of planting

Determining the best time for planting siberian irises in one's particular circumstances is an important first step. Early fall is the traditional preference, but spring is recommended by others, and some gardeners lately have selected the period immediately after the end of bloom as the best. In fact, the best time depends chiefly on the geographic location and climatic condition of the garden. In the north, planting after early September is inadvisable because cold weather stops root growth before the plant is anchored in place; even if deeply mulched, the plant is at risk of being heaved out of the ground by subsequent freezes and thaws. In such northern climates, with their mild summers and usually fairly frequent rain, spring planting is unquestionably better. In contrast, spring planting in the south subjects the newly set plants to long, hot, dry summers, with many plants inevitably lost (Luihn 1973), whereas late fall planting is followed by several months of good growing conditions and a mild winter.

An argument in favor of planting and transplanting shortly after bloom is that at that time, new roots and rhizomes are actively growing, and the newly divided plants quickly start vigorous growth, with fair probability that they will bloom the next year. Obviously, this timing is suitable only in regions where other conditions, such as relatively cool weather and abundant water, can be relied upon. Siberian irises planted in the spring may be expected to bloom the following year but very rarely the same year. If planted in the fall, bloom cannot be expected until the second year.

Planting

Siberian irises will do quite well if one merely digs a hole in the bed, puts the plant in it, replaces the dirt, and waters copiously, but those who take extra pains in planting are rewarded by the improved performance of the plants. The procedure varies, depending on whether a few plants are to be added to an existing perennial bed, or if a large number of plants are to be set in a newly prepared bed. For the perennial bed, dig a hole large enough to receive the plant without crowding the roots and at least 10 inches (25 centimeters) deep. Mix a large trowel full of thoroughly composted manure well into the soil at the bottom of the hole. Make a mound of dirt at the bottom of the hole; place the plant on the mound and spread the roots down around the mound. Fill back in with dirt to which compost has been added. The height of the mound should be such that when the plant is placed on it, the crown (where the leaves emerge from the rhizome) will be 1.5 to 2 inches (3.5 to 5 centimeters) below the final level of the soil when the plant is in place (Figure 5-1). Water abundantly, or even better, apply a weak solution of a root-stimulating hormone, such as a naphthylacetic acid mixture (see Table 5-2) of 1 teaspoon (5 milliliters) per gallon (3.8 liters) of water. Note: Stronger solutions are sometimes recommended but can lead to distorted development of the leaves. In the rare instance of a plant known to be susceptible to botrytis infection, half a teaspoon (2.5 milliliters) of benomyl (see Table 6-1) may also be added to each gallon (3.8 liters) of water.

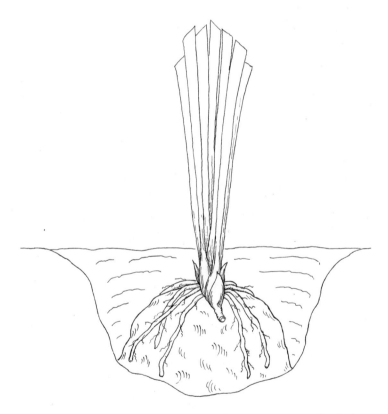

Figure 5-1. Method of planting, with crown properly below ground level.

The procedure for planting many siberian irises in rows, as for a display or seedling bed, is different. Dig a wide trench to a depth of 10 inches (25 centimeters) or more, with well-composted manure and other organic material thoroughly dug into the bottom. Fill back in with the removed dirt. If the number of plants is not so large as to make the extra effort unreasonable, double digging is still better. Place the top layer of soil on one side of the trench and the lower layer of soil on the other side. Thoroughly dig composted manure into the bottom of the trench along its entire length. Next, fill the topsoil back in. Mix the subsoil with compost; use it, together with some fresh soil if needed, to finish filling the trench. Planting can be done at once or at any time later.

With either method, carefully prepare the plants to be used. Cut leaves back to 6 to 8 inches (15 to 20 centimeters), except those small seedlings that have just been removed from their flats or pots. Wash the roots, and cut out dead or damaged roots and rhizomes. Examine the rootstock closely if the plant has come from a bed where it might have been contaminated with grass or weed roots; remove any that are found.

It is essential that the roots be kept moist. One can expect that plants received from a distance will be well packed with wet sphagnum moss or paper towels around the roots in a plastic bag. Even so, it is wise to soak the roots of all plants in water for several hours before planting, even those dug from one's own garden.

Transplanting

This is essentially the same as planting newly received plants, the only differences having to do with the size of the plants. Average-sized clumps should be dug with a spading fork, to minimize damage to the roots. Very large clumps may be dug with a spade; a few cut roots may result, but this is a small price to pay for the greater leverage a spade provides. Once out of the ground, the clump usually needs to be divided, which is easily done. Insert two spading forks, back to back, at the center of the clump and down through the roots. Draw their handles apart and then force them together, separating the clump into two halves. Create further subdivisions in the same way. Wash away dirt from the divisions with the jet stream of a hose, and remove old, spent rhizomes and roots. In old clumps, much of the central part should be discarded and only the young, peripheral portions replanted. The divisions thus obtained are planted in the same way as are new plants.

Water

Once the 28-chromosome cultivars and the tetraploids derived from them become established, they withstand relatively dry conditions as well as most perennial flowers, but for the first few months after transplanting they should not be allowed to become dry. This is absolutely essential. Even after they are fully established, they should have at least 1 inch (2.5 centimeters) of water weekly. If rainfall is not sufficient, the hose or other means of watering can provide the balance.

Fertilizer

Fertilizer should not be applied until approximately three weeks after planting. For established plants, work a handful or so per plant of ordinary granular fertilizer into the soil along the rows when growth starts in the spring, and then again at the end of bloom. Fertilizers with formulas containing 10 percent nitrogen, 10 percent phosphorus, and 10 percent potassium (commonly expressed as 10–10–10) are often used, but different gardeners use different formulas, all with good results. For my part, I send soil samples to our local University Cooperative Extension Service for analysis and follow their recommendations. Some growers rely entirely on soluble fertilizer, making two applications in the spring, a third before bloom, a fourth just after bloom, and a fifth in early autumn. I rely chiefly on granular fertilizer, using soluble fertilizer—in one or two booster applications—only to improve the performance of plants that are growing poorly and to increase stock of particularly needed seedlings.

An additional comment regarding phosphorous: Robert Hollingworth warns that it is very immobile in the soil, and that when applied on the surface as a component of granular fertilizer, little of it reaches the roots. Hence, in preparing a bed for planting, he spreads fertilizer high in phosphorus (15–35–15) just before the final tilling, and then tills it in deeply. Such a fertilizer can be made by thoroughly mixing a granular 15–15–15 fertilizer with an equal amount of superphosphate (R. M. Hollingworth 1994).

The utility of composted manures, animal and otherwise, does not end with the preparation of the bed and subsequent planting. They also serve excellently to supplement chemical fertilizers or, used with other organic fertilizers, to replace them. Mototeru Kamo, a Japanese grower,

Table 5-1. Average nutrient percentages of manures and organic fertilizers; all figures are per 100 pounds.

	Nitrogen (N)	Phosphorus (P)	Potassium (K)
Fresh cow manure with bedding	.5 lb	.3 lb	.5 lb
Dried poultry manure without litter	4.0 lbs	3.0 lbs	3.0 lbs
Dried rabbit manure without bedding	2.4 lbs	.6 lb	.05 lb
Fresh sheep manure	1.0 lb	.4 lb	.2 lb
Fresh horse manure	.4 lb	.2 lb	.4 lb
Blood meal	15.0 lbs	1.3 lbs	.7 lb
Bone meal	4.0 lbs	21.0 lbs	.2 lb
Cottonseed meal	3.2 lbs	1.3 lbs	1.2 lbs
Farrowing swine manure	4.0 lbs	1.0 lb	negligible

The composting of fresh manures often lowers their nutrient content because of leaching; well-managed composting can significantly raise nutrient levels, however, as initial water-to-solid-material ratio is reduced. (Fresh manure contains a large amount of water.) Adapted from the Brooklyn Botanic Garden's *Soils Handbook No. 10* (1990).

spreads composted cow manure about 1 inch (2.5 centimeters) thick between the rows at time of planting and again after bloom to serve as a mulch as well as a fertilizer. Alternatively, he recommends applying the composted manure some 3 inches (7.5 centimeters) thick between the rows in early spring and tilling it into the soil when the leaves are 6 to 8 inches (15 to 20 centimeters) tall (Kamo 1989; McEwen 1991).

Table 5-1 summarizes the percentages of various nutrients in several organic materials used as fertilizers. The various animal manures differ quite markedly. Blood meal is the highest in nitrogen and bone meal in phosphorus. Of the less commonly used materials, I have detailed information only for cottonseed meal used in conjunction with ordinary 10–10–10 granular fertilizer. Burton (1993) recommends scattering cottonseed meal liberally around the plants when growth starts in the spring to within 4 inches (10 centimeters) of the plants, but no closer. It must be thoroughly raked into the soil and then thoroughly watered; if that is not done, a crust forms on the soil surface that is almost impenetrable by water. Approximately three weeks later, the 10–10–10 fertilizer is applied. The cottonseed meal and fertilizer are applied similarly once more, after bloom or in the early fall.

Weeds and their control

For the homeowner with a small, intimate garden, the recurring need for weeding can be one of the actually pleasant rites of spring (and summer and fall), giving a sense of contact with the soil and the satisfaction of playing such a personal role in the care of the flowers. For most, however, and especially for those with very large gardens, weeding is an extremely tedious task and the most expensive in terms of time and labor costs.

From the standpoint of the horticulturist, many specific plants in the garden behave as weeds. From the standpoint of the gardener, any plant growing in the garden that is not wanted and interferes with the desired plants may be thought of as a weed. In a general sense, the gardener has always differentiated between grass-type weeds and the broad-leaf types, but because dealing with them required the same physical measures of hand or tool cultivation and mulching, there was little need to distinguish between the two. With the development of herbicides for particular purposes, however, the distinction has become of very practical importance.

Table 5-2 lists a number of available herbicides. This is such an active field of research and development that there will inevitably be new and presumably improved ones to join their ranks. The table gives both the common (generic) names and the trade names of the products and notes their particular use. A common name is the officially approved one; the trade names are those given to the product by the manufacturers. Only one common name is assigned a given material, but what is essentially the same product may be sold under a variety of different trade names, depending on the manufacturers who make it. Trade names are always capitalized; common names are not. Only common names are used in the text of this book, but readers can refer to Table 5-2 to find the trade names, which may be easier to identify in garden stores.

Before discussing the new and, indeed, also the older herbicides, I must emphasize that all must be used with care—care to protect not only the irises but also oneself and the environment. The directions provided by the manufacturers must be strictly followed. Finally, it is always

Table 5-2. Herbicides and growth stimulants.

Common name	Trade name	Type
Herbicides		
benefin	Balan	nonselective preemergent
fluazifop-P-butyl	Fusilade, Ornamec	grass-specific postemergent
glyphosate	Roundup, Kleenup	nonselective postemergent
isoxaben	Snapshot,[a] Gallery	nonselective preemergent
sethoxydim	Vantage, Poast	grass-specific postemergent
simazine	Simazine	nonselective preemergent
trifluralin	Treflan	nonselective preemergent
Growth stimulants		
naphthylacetic acid	Superthrive,[a] Rootone[a]	

[a] Contains other ingredients also.

wise to try any new product on a trial area first before using it widely throughout the iris garden, unless the benefits as well as the possible injurious effects of the product are fully known.

The herbicides used for the control of weeds fall into three broad groups: those indiscriminate killers that are lethal to all plants, those that selectively kill grass-type weeds, and those that selectively kill broad-leaf weeds. Herbicides are also of pre- and postemergent type. The nonselective herbicides, such as glyphosate, are of particular value in preparing a new area for garden use, as they kill grass, weeds, and plants of all kinds. Such herbicides have been available for many years, but earlier ones have been removed from the market. They were environmentally harmful and tended to remain at lethal levels in the soil, making it unsafe to use the garden for a year or even longer. Glyphosate, on the other hand, is effective only while in the plant; its action is lost in the soil. Hence the cleared area can be dug and prepared for garden use in about a week. Some experienced gardeners with large areas to weed sometimes use glyphosate between the rows of their irises, but they do so only with great care and on windless days (Aitken 1994). This practice cannot, however, be recommended to most amateur gardeners. Glyphosate kills even such difficult weeds as crab grass but not clover, which Aitken, after trial of other herbicides, prefers to weed by hand.

Preemergent weed killers, such as trifluralin and simazine, have been available for many years also. They are unquestionably effective, but the experiences of many highly skilled owners of important nurseries lead to the conclusion that they can cause significant damage to irises. Several new preemergent herbicides are becoming available, some of which appear to be especially promising in control of broad-leaf weeds. As with any new control measure, try them on a test area for at least a season before using them on a wide scale.

Controlled trials of a dozen or more of the newer agents have been carried out at the University of Minnesota since 1990 (Swanson et al 1993). The various materials have been evaluated as to their effectiveness in controlling weeds and their effect on the quality of the iris. Unfortunately—and perhaps as might be expected—some of the most effective were also most harmful to the irises. None was as effective in controlling the weeds as was a 4 to 6 inch (10 to 15 centimeter) mulch of wood chips. Of the chemical agents, benefin resulted in a tenfold reduction in the number of weeds (compared with an unweeded control area) and appeared to cause no harm to the siberian irises. Indeed, in that respect, the siberian irises treated with benefin did better than those with wood chip mulch and those in a control bed weeded simply by cultivation. This study also clearly demonstrated the deleterious effect of weeds. The irises in the nonweeded control area suffered significantly as the season advanced and the weeds grew. This important study is encouraging and gives hope that an effective control of broad-leaf weeds may be on the way. Of course, it is too early to be sure that continued use of such agents will not lead to accumulative injury to the irises.

Turning to the grass-type weeds, one finds the situation very promising indeed. Several herbicides specific for grass-type weeds have been in use for several years. In the University of Minnesota trials described above, the grass-specific herbicide sethoxydim was extremely effective and appeared to cause no harm. Still more encouraging are the excellent results reported by experienced gardeners who have used sethoxydim as a grass-specific herbicide for two to five years (Bauer and Coble 1994; R. M. Hollingworth 1994; Wadekamper 1994). They report that it can be applied directly to the grass-infested iris clump without harm to the irises themselves.

We have at last reason to hope that the age-old problem of weed control may soon be solved. Meanwhile, the time-honored measures of mulching and cultivation and the use of cover crops help the hard pressed gardener.

Mulches

Mulches are extremely useful in the garden for three reasons: they control weeds, they conserve water in the soil, and they provide winter protection. Many different organic materials serve as mulches, including pine needles, shredded leaves, wood chips, pine bark, cocoa and buck-wheat hulls, and straw. Straw of various sorts is especially valuable in large plantings, such as seedling and commercial gardens, where its less attractive appearance is of minor concern. Salt hay is ideal as it lacks weed seeds, but it is expensive and often is not easily found. Oat straw is also useful but should be purchased only if the oats were harvested before the straw was baled. In the north—that is to say in places where the winter temperature falls below 20 degrees Fahrenheit (–7 degrees Celsius)—the oat seedlings that sprout from straw spread in the garden in late fall present no problem as they will be killed by the ensuing cold, but oat straw spread in the spring can be very troublesome if full of oats. Wheat straw also is good, but only if it has been well threshed since wheat seedlings are winter hardy. Fortunately any pending problem from sprouted oats or wheat kernels can be readily controlled with sethoxydim or another of the grass-specific herbicides without harm to the irises.

A mulch of plastic sheeting is an excellent way to control weeds and conserve moisture but provides no winter protection. In areas of high winds the sheets must be stapled in place; if not, they can be torn or whipped about, injuring the irises. Modern plastic sheets allow rain to soak through and are strong enough to last several years, but when they are no longer useful, they must be discarded, whereas the spent, partly rotted organic mulches can be tilled in to improve the soil.

Valuable as they are, mulches have their negative aspects. The application of heavy mulches, such as bark chips, can interfere with water flow and encourages growth of fungi. Mulches can complicate pest control in places where slugs or field mice are a problem. A mulch of straw is easily lifted to reveal the slugs enjoying the moist conditions underneath, but this is more difficult with a mulch of stapled-down plastic sheets.

Weed control: Mulching with organic material or plastic sheets greatly reduces the number of troublesome weed invaders. A layer of oat straw or other material 3 inches (7.5 centimeters) thick is adequate. Such weeds as do appear cannot be removed by cultivating or tilling, but the number should not be large and they can easily be removed by hand. Furthermore, as nearly all weeds crop up adjacent to or in the iris clumps, only hand weeding would be possible in any event, mulch or no mulch.

Conservation of water: The second important use of mulches is to conserve moisture in the soil, as scientific studies clearly confirm. The water content of unmulched soil varies greatly, with large amounts present after rain and much less between storms. In contrast, except in long periods of drought, the water content of mulched soil remains adequate and fairly constant. Siberian irises greatly appreciate this.

Winter protection: Mature, established 28-chromosome siberian irises are so winter hardy that they do not need winter protection, but mulches may be helpful in saving plants that go into the winter in a condition weakened through disease or injury. In places where the winter temperature can be expected to go below freezing, small seedlings planted in spring should be mulched because their relatively short roots cannot anchor them during the subsequent winter's freezes and thaws. Likewise even mature clumps planted late in the fall will require a winter mulch; they too will have made insufficient root growth to resist heaving that first winter. The optimum depth of mulch depends on the severity of cold expected and how widely the temperature varies during the winter. In areas where a good snow cover can be relied on, less organic mulch is necessary. In our hybridizing garden in mid-coastal Maine, the winter temperature can reach −15 degrees Fahrenheit (−26 degrees Celsius); here, 10 inches (25 centimeters) of oat straw is required. Before the mulch is put on, browning leaves are cut off and removed to get rid of plant material that might harbor pest or disease agents. In the spring, the straw is raked from the plants to the paths between the rows, where—with some fresh straw, if needed—it helps to control weeds and keep the soil moist. After three years, when that seedling bed must be emptied to make room for a new crop of seedlings, the old straw is tilled into the soil.

Green manures and soil additives

Green manures, or cover crops, are grown on fallow ground and tilled in to improve the physical structure of the soil. The microorganisms that break green manures down themselves take nutrients from the soil, but new nutrients are given back as decomposition continues. A variety of plants are used in this way, including those that add nitrogen to the soil, such as some clovers and legumes; many, such as winter rye and buckwheat, are primarily soil conditioners, adding organic matter to improve soil texture. I have found buckwheat particularly useful because it matures so quickly that several crops can be tilled in during a single growing season. The last crop of buckwheat is followed by winter rye, which grows all winter and is tilled into the soil in the spring when the bed is prepared for planting.

Soil additives, among them manure, compost, peat moss, and sand, are called for in the earliest stage of culture, the preparation of the bed. Peat moss, especially hypnum-moss, is a very good soil conditioner that also has nutritive value. Vermiculite and perlite—while excellent as ingredients of growing mediums to start seeds—are not suitable as soil conditioners; they lack structural strength, become crushed in garden soil, and can impede drainage. Polymer gels, which materials absorb and hold water for slow release, are also employed as soil additives. They are interesting but expensive, and their value is not yet established.

Alfalfa, chiefly in the form of pellets, has been used for years and has aroused the interest and enthusiasm of several experienced growers of various types of irises. Some use it together with granular fertilizers, but others depend on it alone. To prepare a bed for planting, scatter the pellets rather thickly at the rate of 50 pounds (23 kilograms) per 100 feet (30 meters) of row and then till them into the soil. After the plants are in place, scatter alfalfa pellets along the rows at approximately the same rate, and repeat monthly throughout the growing season. The pellets soon absorb water and disintegrate into the soil. Even with a mulch in place, the pellets will work themselves into the soil and need not be scratched in. They cause no apparent harm even if in contact with the plant (Varner 1992; Aitken 1994; Markham 1994).

Assuming that alfalfa does indeed result in stronger growth and improved plants, one may reasonably wonder how these benefits are brought about. Alfalfa contains triacontanol, a plant growth stimulant. Some studies report increased growth rates when triacontanol is applied to plants in weak concentration; other studies report failures (R. M. Hollingworth 1991). Alfalfa also contains several vitamins, trace metals, and other chemical substances. Aitken (1994) suggests that one major function of the alfalfa pellets may be to replace whatever has been lost in the iris beds from the prolonged growing of a single type of plant. Certainly it is too early to do more than speculate on how alfalfa works or, indeed, to state with confidence just how valuable it is, but it appears promising.

I close this discussion of soil additives and conditioners with one caution: Although tilling is an extremely efficient means of mixing all types of green manures and additives into the soil, the weight of the machine and the person guiding it tend to cause compaction of the soil's deeper layers. Tilling should therefore be done no more than is necessary to accomplish the mixing.

Subsequent care

Throughout the summer, proper attention must be paid to watering and to weed control. If the paths between rows are not covered with mulch, cultivate sufficiently to control weeds and to keep the soil around the plants loose and aerated. If the paths are mulched, weed by hand. Control grass-type weeds with selective herbicides, such as sethoxydim.

As unwanted seed pods form, cut off the stalks bearing them as low as possible and discard. Some gardeners with perennial and display beds like to let these pods remain and grow larger, which adds to the interest of the plants when bloom has ended, but this carries with it a responsibility. Such pods must be watched closely and cut off before they spill seeds; failure to do so can result in seedlings that are not what the plant marker proclaims. Naturally the hybridizer has different plans for pods; those special concerns are addressed in Chapters 8 and 10.

Allow leaves to remain on the plants as long as they are green and adding energy to the plant through photosynthesis. When they turn brown in the fall, cut them off as low as possible and burn them. It is risky to add them to the compost pile, as they may carry fungal spores, insect eggs, and other disease agents.

Fall is the time to sow an overwinter cover crop, such as winter rye, to be tilled into the soil the following spring. If the situation calls for it, a winter mulch is best put on after the ground freezes, as the purpose of the mulch is chiefly to prevent the plants from being heaved during freezes and thaws. Small seedlings planted earlier in spring, which still have only rather short roots, require a winter mulching, as do plants of any size planted in late fall, which will not have had time to make firmly anchoring root growth. Established plants of the 28-chromosome group are fully winter hardy and need no protective mulch.

Finally, this is that great time of the garden year to start making plans for the year ahead.

Long-term care

Every farmer is aware of the need to rotate crops; the gardener often is not. Yet as the years pass, the chief problems in many gardens are those caused by monoculture, the practice of growing a single crop in the same soil, year after year. The typical home gardener has no cause for concern because the mixed bed is planted with a variety of perennials and annuals, but the situation is different for the hybridizer or collector who specializes in a single type of plant and grows it year after year, without admixture of other plants. If they have ample space, such gardeners can always arrange to have fallow areas that can be planted to other crops, such as vegetables, or can use cover crops as described in the preceding section.

The long-term deleterious effects of monoculture are well known, yet no cause or causes have been clearly proven. One may speculate about the possibilities: the disturbance of the balance of microorganisms in the soil; the gradual removal by the plants of substances essential to their growth; and the accumulation in the soil of substances harmful to the plants, either through waste products from the plants themselves or from materials such as fertilizers, sprays, and the like. Senescent changes in plants left in place too long contribute significantly to their deterioration.

Rotation of crops is the best way to avoid soil deterioration. Where lack of space or other factors prevent rotation, one must rely on other measures—which, indeed, should be used even where crop rotation is possible. These include a deep tilling of the soil together with an application of composted manure before replanting; ample watering combined with good drainage; and continued application of natural fertilizers, such as composted manures and other composts. The effects of senescence can be avoided by dividing and replanting the plants every three years, and continuous addition of new soil and removal of some old soil can be accomplished, at least in part, by discarding the ball of soil that clings to the roots when a plant is lifted and adding new soil to replace it. Aitken (1994) suggests that alfalfa pellets may supply necessary nutrients lost through monoculture. Finally, if serious disease problems occur, empty that area of the garden and treat with dazomet, metam-sodium, or some other soil fumigant; add some new soil and compost before replanting.

Subseries *Chrysographes*

In general, cultural requirements of the 40-chromosome group of siberian irises are the same as those of the 28-chromosome group, but most gardeners find them less easy to grow. Although they are reported to need acid soil with a preferred pH of approximately 5.8 (McGarvey 1975), they grow extremely well in an Oregon garden with pH 5.0 (Reid 1991) and in an English garden with a pH of 7.5 (Hewitt 1990). More strongly alkaline conditions should be avoided. Just as for the 28-chromosome siberian irises, ample water is required, a minimum of 1 inch (2.5 centimeters) weekly. Helsley (1983) floods his 40-chromosome siberian irises for a few hours every three or four days through the growing season if it does not rain.

Experience indicates that climatic factors are more significant for these siberian irises than for the 28-chromosome cultivars. James Waddick points out that all 40-chromosome species are native to high altitudes near tropics, where they are exposed to neither excessively high nor excessively low temperatures; in their native element, the summers are cool and the winters mild, with ample rainfall and high humidity (Waddick and Zhao 1992). In our garden in Maine the summer temperatures are ideal, but those in winter can reach −15 degrees Fahrenheit (−26 degrees Celsius). Here, even established clumps of some 40-chromosome hybrids and tetraploids can be lost if not heavily mulched in winter.

Growing Siberian Irises in Pots

Siberian irises can be grown in pots, but this is usually done for a specific purpose. Pot culture is used for plants that are to be moved without a prepared bed's being ready to receive them; for the temporary care of sick plants, or of plants arriving in cold areas too early for planting out of doors; and for forcing and retarding bloom.

Fill pots of a size appropriate for the plant with your preferred potting mix. I use a mix of equal parts garden loam and well-seasoned compost. Cut the leaves back, just as when preparing plants for the garden bed. Apply no fertilizer until vigorous growth is apparent. If the plant is to remain in the pot for more than a few days and if the ground is not frozen, bury the pot in the ground.

Forcing and retarding bloom

Frequently, one would like to display siberian or other irises at a flower show scheduled for a date when they are not normally in bloom. Potted japanese irises brought indoors under lights at a temperature of 50 degrees Fahrenheit (10 degrees Celsius) can be expected to bloom in eighty to ninety days (Ito 1966; Hirao 1984). Warner (1992) used roughly the same procedure to force bloom in siberian and other irises. The siberian irises were lifted, potted, and placed in a refrigerator at a little above freezing in late October. Since siberian irises bloom about a month earlier than japanese irises, they were brought into a greenhouse approximately fifty-five days before the desired date of bloom. The temperature was kept at 55 degrees Fahrenheit (13 degrees Celsius), and the natural sunlight was augmented with four to ten additional hours of artificial light. Most of the siberian irises bloomed satisfactorily in time for the flower show, but the leaves were longer and less firm than normal. Clearly a certain amount of guesswork must enter into the decision of when to start the plants in the greenhouse. It would be safest to start a few plants a week or so apart.

Adolph J. Vogt (1987) of Louisville, Kentucky, used refrigeration to store over winter a large number of japanese irises that he had dug in late fall but was unable to plant. He cleaned the plants thoroughly, cut leaves back to 4 or 5 inches (10 or 12 centimeters), placed the entire plant in a sealed, light plastic bag, and stored them in the refrigerator at 40 to 46 degrees Fahrenheit (4 to 8 degrees Celsius). Plants removed and planted the next spring before May grew well; those planted after mid-May did not grow. This method might prove effective with siberian irises also.

Shipping Plants

Shipping is only indirectly a part of culture, but proper transport is essential to ensure the plant's survival and growth in the new garden. It is critical that the roots not be allowed to dry out. For ordinary shipping over distances that will require only a few days to several weeks from door to door, the following procedure is standard.

Dig the plants to be shipped, and cut leaves back to approximately 4 to 5 inches (10 to 12 centimeters). Divide the plant into pieces of the size desired, usually two or three fans per division. Wash the divisions thoroughly with the jet stream of the hose, as it is illegal to ship plants with soil. Examine the clean divisions, and cut out any dead or damaged roots or rhizomes. Wrap the roots and rhizome in wet paper towels, or cover them with wet peat moss. The paper towel or peat moss should be quite moist, but not dripping wet. Place each division in a suitably sized plastic bag, and tie just above the rhizome, leaving the leaves out of the bag. Punch holes approximately 0.25 to 0.5 inch (6 to 12 millimeters) in diameter into the sides of the shipping carton to permit air circulation.

Plants packed in this way should remain in good condition for several weeks, but the sooner they can be replanted the better. Once a shipment I made to Japan became lost and was not received for more than two months. The plants were in sad condition, but with loving care they survived. In situations where slow travel is anticipated, pack the roots and rhizome in wet peat moss held in place with a second wrapping of wet paper towels.

I know of only one bad experience using the standard method just described. An experienced grower in Lithuania frequently lost plants to a form of crown rot in the thirty days or so they took to reach him through the postal service of the former Soviet Union. The problem was solved by having the wet paper towels cover only the roots and distal part of the rhizome. The plastic bag was then tied below the crown and adjacent part of the rhizome, leaving the crown and base of the leaves uncovered (Kondratas 1994).

Chapter 6

Insects
and
Other Pests

Several insects and other pests affect siberian irises. Most are not serious, fortunately, and all are controllable. The most serious, the iris borer, is discussed first, in detail, and the others then more briefly.

Most gardeners know that many of the chemical agents used to control pests and diseases are double-edged swords. As well as being beneficial, they can pose hazards if improperly used—hazards to the environment and to the people working with them. There is indeed a steadily growing interest in using more natural materials and practices, commonly referred to as organic, that do not depend on manufactured chemical agents; nevertheless, synthetic chemical materials are still necessary, and in this chapter and the next, several of these agents are discussed.

I cannot emphasize too strongly: *Chemicals must be used with care and in accordance with the manufacturer's directions and warnings.* If so used on an occasional basis, there is little reason to be concerned about possible hazards. Remember too that it is legal to use these agents only in the amounts and on the specific crops authorized by the U.S. Environmental Protection Agency. Lawful uses are printed on the directions and labels of the products. Unfortunately, irises are not listed for some materials very useful in their culture simply because the manufacturer did not apply to the agency for product registration for use with irises; in this case, irises may be taken to be included under the generic terms "ornamental plants" or "ornamentals."

Table 6-1 lists chemical materials useful in the control of plant pests and diseases. Some of these are not registered by the Environmental Protection Agency for use on ornamentals, but the regulations change frequently, with some compounds dropped from approval and others gaining approval. Any product listed in Table 6-1 that is not presently approved is included because of its probable usefulness and the possibility that it may be registered eventually. If you are uncertain about the proper application of any material mentioned in this book, check with your local Department of Agriculture or your University Cooperative Extension Service.

Table 6-1 gives both common (generic) and trade names as well as the product's activity. Contact pesticides must come in contact with the pest to kill it. They are most effective at the time of application but may remain effective for days or even a week or more, depending on the nature of the product and whether or not there is rain. Systemic pesticides are absorbed by the plant's tissues and kill the pest when it feeds on the plant. They may remain in the tissues at effective levels for a week or more and are not affected by rain. Systemic pesticides are especially useful to kill insects and fungi that are deep in the tissues of the plant and cannot be effectively reached by contact sprays. The products that con-

Table 6-1. Names and types of materials for control of plant problems.

Common name	Trade name	Type
Insecticides		
acephate	Orthene	systemic
Bacillus thuringiensis products	Dipel, Thuricide Bactospeine	stomach poison[a]
bifenthrin	Talstar, Attain	contact
carbaryl	Sevin	contact
chlorpyrifos	Dursban, Lorsban	contact
cyfluthrin	Tempo, Baythroid	contact
diatomaceous earth		
diazinon	Diazinon	contact
diflubenzuron	Dimilin	contact
dimethoate	Cygon 2E, Rogor	systemic

Common name	Trade name	Type
disulfoton	Di-syston, Dithiosytox	systemic
fatty acid salts	Safer soaps	contact
fenvalerate or esfenvalerate	Pydrin, Sumicidin, Asana	contact
fluvalinate	Mavrik	contact
lindane	Lindane	contact-
malathion	Cythion, Malathion	contact
neem extract	Margosan-O	stomach poison[a]
oxamyl	Vydate	systemic
permethrin	Ambush, Pounce, Talcord	contact
pyrethrum	many names	contact

Fungicides

benomyl	Tersan	systemic
captan	Captan	contact
maneb	Manzate	contact
metalaxyl	Subdue, Ridomil	systemic
oxycarboxin	Plantvax	systemic
quintozene	PCNB, Terraclor	contact
thiophanate-methyl	Cleary 3336, Domain, Banrot	systemic
thiram	Dilsan, Mercuram, Thimesite	contact
triadimefon	Bayleton	systemic
triforine	Funginex	systemic

Nematicides

ethoprop	Mocap	contact
fenamiphos	Nemacur	contact

Soil fumigants

dazomet	Basamid	
metam-sodium	Vapam	

[a] Must be ingested by the insect.

tain *Bacillus thuringiensis* are in a special category; they are not absorbed by the plant, nor do they penetrate the insect's cuticle, so are neither strictly systemic nor strictly contact. Rather, they must be ingested by the pest in order to kill it.

In preparation for writing this book, I sent a detailed questionnaire to experienced iris growers in the United States and other countries, asking for their experiences with various pests and diseases and specifically requesting information regarding these problems in siberian irises of subseries *Sibiricae* and *Chrysographes*, tall bearded irises, *Iris versicolor*, and japanese irises. I received replies from eighteen growers altogether: fourteen from widely scattered regions in this country, two from England, and one each from Belgium and Germany. The specific information obtained in this way augments the general discussion of the various pest and disease problems in this chapter and the next. I am greatly indebted to all the friends who provided this extremely useful information.

Iris Borer

For reasons that remain unclear, the iris borer is of little if any concern in the southern United States and west of the Rocky Mountains and is unknown in England and the Continent. In the rest of the United States, however, it is a serious pest, affecting irises of all types, a situation that was fully borne out in the responses to our questionnaire. Iris borers are also reported in Japan but may be a different species since in the United States the life cycle permits only one generation a year, whereas in Japan several generations appear in a single year (Kamo 1989; Horinaka 1994).

The borer is the larva of *Macronoctua onusta*, a brownish, night-flying moth. The species we know in the United States goes through four stages in its life cycle: egg, larva, pupa, and moth. (For excellent pictures of the borer in each stage, see Naegele 1959.) In the fall the moth lays its eggs on leaves and stalks and organic debris around the plants. In the spring the eggs hatch, and the tiny larvae soon climb up the new leaves and chew their way into them. From there they gradually eat their way down to the rhizomes. At that stage the larva is 0.10 to 0.25 inch (3 to 6 millimeters) long but by August has grown to 1.5 inches (3.5 centimeters) long and 0.5 inch (1 centimeter) wide. This growth has been made at the expense of the rhizome, which is hollowed out and destroyed. Indeed, in siberian irises the small rhizome is soon devoured, and the borer moves quickly into another, with the result that a large part of the clump can be destroyed.

The larva is easily identified. It is a hairless, light gray, segmented caterpillar with pinkish tones and a dark brown head. In Maine the mature larva becomes a pupa around mid-August and leaves the rhizome to pupate in the ground near the plant. In southern regions this stage is reached earlier. After approximately a month the pupa becomes a mature moth, which emerges to lay its eggs—and the cycle starts again. The moth is about 1 inch (2.5 centimeters) long, an inconspicuous dark brown in color with lighter brown wings, but is rarely seen, as it flies at night.

Close examination of the leaf edges in the spring may reveal the telltale, saw-toothed holes made by the larvae as they eat their way into the leaves. The small entrance lesions are less easily found in the slender leaves of siberian irises than in the wider leaves of tall bearded irises. If holes are found, squeeze the leaves firmly from the entry point to their bases; this may kill the larvae. The next evidence of borer damage is the appearance of yellowing leaves at the center of the plant, but by that time considerable damage will have been done. The yellowed leaves are easily pulled free at the base, revealing a chewed and usually blackened end. To destroy the borer, insert a wire where the leaf came away and move it about in the rhizome, or enlarge the hole enough to accommodate a pencil-sized piece of wood and perform the same action. As an additional measure, the plant can be heavily sprayed with dimethoate. If in a few weeks the plant continues to show yellowing of new central leaves, it is best to lift the plant, cut into the rhizome, and identify the borer, which by that time will be large enough to be easily spotted. Since the larvae are cannibalistic, only one will be found in a rhizome, but make a thorough search for borers in other rhizomes before the iris is replanted.

By late summer the larvae will have left the rhizome, and only the hollowed-out shell of the rhizome will remain. At that stage, look carefully through the top few inches of soil all around the plant, for a radius of about 10 inches (25 centimeters), to uncover any pupae. They are easily identified: oval and shiny, approximately 0.5 to 1 inch (1 to 2.5 centimeters) long, and chestnut-brown in color. The search is best made with the aid of a coarse sieve. Killing the pupae cannot undo the damage already caused but is helpful in reducing the borer population in the next year.

In addition to these direct lethal steps, the control of iris borers demands a series of preventive measures. First is the late fall clean-up of the garden. Removing the iris leaves and debris around the plants gets rid of borer eggs laid there by the moths, which will greatly reduce the number of larvae the following spring. All leaves and debris should then be burned.

A spray program in the spring using the systemic insecticide dimethoate is also very effective against iris borers. Mix 1 tablespoon (15 milliliters) of dimethoate per gallon (3.8 liters) of water together with a few drops of spreading agent, and spray the base of the plant thoroughly with the mixture when the leaves are approximately 4 inches (10 centimeters) tall. The entire leaf area need not be sprayed, as the dimethoate is absorbed and is carried throughout the plant in the xylem. Too heavy a spraying of the upper leaves can cause leaf tip burn, especially in hot weather. If borer damage was severe the previous year, spray a second time a week or ten days after the first application. After a year or two, if no further borer damage occurs, the spray can be reduced to once yearly and then stopped, but a close watch must be kept and the program resumed if borers reappear.

Other systemic pesticides, such as acephate and disulfoton, are effective, but some growers have found continued application of acephate harmful to the irises, and disulfoton is more toxic to the user than dimethoate and should be used with even more caution. Nonsystemic sprays, such as lindane, malathion, fenvalerate, and permethrin, can be used instead of dimethoate, but this requires repeated weekly application from the time growth starts in the spring until the leaves are about 12 inches (30 centimeters) tall.

Several biological and organic measures are used against borers, but my experience with them is limited. Diatomaceous earth scattered on the ground around the plant and on the leaves from the start of growth to a height of 12 inches (30 centimeters) may kill the small larvae as they crawl across the ground and up the leaves prior to entering them. The dustings must be repeated after a rain. Spines present in diatomaceous earth pierce the soft tissues of the larvae, causing them to dehydrate; hence the unrefined product is employed, not the type used in swimming pool filters. Although not chemically toxic, diatomaceous earth can cause severe irritation to throat and lungs, and the user should wear a respirator when applying it. Actual evidence of significant usefulness is meager.

Another organic approach is the use of juvenile parasitic nematodes of the family Steinernamatidae (*Steinernema carpocapsal*) and others. These beneficial nematodes live in the soil and parasitize a host of mature insects and their larvae and pupae. They attack more than 250 insect pests, including—besides iris borers—cutworms, corn root worms, european corn borers, japanese beetle larvae, webworms, termites, and many others. They enter the larva or pupa, kill it in twenty-four to forty-eight hours, and then reproduce within their victim, thus continuing their population in the soil. Since they are soil-dwellers, nematodes can attack borer larvae only in the short time between the larvae's emergence from the egg and the start of their ascent up the leaves. If they succeed in maintaining themselves in the soil, however, nematodes can be effective again when the pupae enter the soil. For application, disperse the nematodes in water and sprinkle on the ground with a watering can at the rate recommended by the provider. Since nematodes are inactivated by bright sunlight, the sprinkling should be done at twilight or on a foggy day. After the sprinkling, water them more deeply into the soil. In warm climates nematodes should establish a continuing population, but where temperatures reach freezing level they are killed and must be reapplied each spring. My experience with them is too short to permit a firm appraisal of their value, but nematodes appear to be promising allies in the fight to control iris borers.

Pesticides derived from *Bacillus thuringiensis* should also be effective against the immature larvae, but tests have not shown them to be very successful in controlling borers. Since they must be ingested to be lethal and are not absorbed by the plant systemically, they can be effective only for the brief period when the larva is chewing its way into the leaf. Ryania, the ground-up root of a South American bush, theoretically should be effective also, but since it, like the *Bacillus thuringiensis* products, must be ingested to kill the borer, it has the same limitation.

Enemies of the Hybridizer

Some pests, although they cause no great harm to the plant, are a concern to the gardener because they spoil the beauty of the flowers. They are a most particular problem to the hybridizer, however, because they destroy anthers, styles, and seeds.

Anther and style destroyers

An unusual fly and several rather common garden pests, such as japanese beetles, earwigs, corn ear worms, and borers, are chief among the attackers of anthers and styles.

Iris bud fly (*Orthochaeta dissimilis*): The iris bud fly was reported by Tiffney (1978) in a Massachusetts garden and subsequently in other parts of that state. It appears to be increasing in Maine, and in our recent survey it was reported in siberian irises in Massachusetts, Belgium, and Germany. In his original description, Malloch (1924) reported it as having been identified also in Connecticut, Illinois, Ohio, and Virginia, and Hoebeke (1994a) puts it in western New York as well. Clearly it is more widespread than had been thought. Hoebeke (1994b) holds that *Orthochaeta dissimilis* occurs only in North America and suspects that a related fly species (*Acklandea servadeii*) damages irises in Europe, where it is known as the iris flower bud fly.

The larva of *Orthochaeta dissimilis* is a white maggot approximately 0.10 inch (3 millimeters) long, cone-shaped, smooth, and white, with a small black dot at the pointed end and the larger end rather flat. Presence of the iris bud fly is first evident when an apparently normal bud opens to reveal ragged, chewed standards and styles. A careful search conducted just after the flower opens may turn up the larva, hidden under the damaged styles. Only a few hours later the larva will be gone, having crawled or dropped down into the spathes. Rarely it may invade the ovary before settling in the spathes, where it pupates and remains over winter; the adult fly emerges the next spring. Dimethoate is effective applied at the same rate as for borer control, except that plants should be sprayed just as the earliest siberian irises form buds. If infected flowers are found, cut off the stalks bearing affected flowers well below the spathes and burn them.

Japanese beetle (*Popillia japonica*): The japanese beetle was reported as a problem in only one Massachusetts garden, where this common garden pest chiefly affected the late bloomers. As in other flowers, the beetles were especially attracted to white blossoms, going first to the anthers and stigmas but quickly shredding the entire blossom. For control, establish a population of parasitic nematodes.

Earwig (*Forficula auricularis*): The earwig was recorded as present in all gardens but troublesome in only one. In our garden in Maine, earwigs are a major problem year after year in japanese irises but do not attack the siberian irises. Perhaps this is a matter of timing, as the japanese irises bloom approximately one month after the siberians. Because of its size, the earwig is readily seen after the damaged flower opens and can be caught with long, slender tweezers. They can also be controlled by dusting carbaryl on the plant and the ground around it.

Corn ear worm: The corn ear worm was reported in siberian irises in only one garden in southern California. If dimethoate or juvenile parasitic nematodes were applied for iris borer control, they should protect against these insects also.

Iris borer: The serious damage caused by the larvae of the iris borer in the rhizomes of irises has already been discussed, but these insects can also be a relatively rare cause of damage to the anthers and styles and can even cut into a stalk, causing it to break off with loss of buds and seed pods. This was noted as a problem in one garden in California and one in Michigan.

Seed destroyers

Two insects specifically destroy seeds within the pods, namely the iris weevil and the verbena bud moth.

Iris weevil or snout beetle (*Mononychus vulpeculus*): The rotund, dark brownish gray iris weevil, less than 0.25 inch (6 millimeters) long, has a snout or beak with which it pierces the walls of the ovary to deposit its eggs. Both the larva and the pupa of this beetle develop inside the pod, where they feed upon the seeds. The adults can also eat anthers and styles, but chief damage is caused inside the pods by the larvae. When the seed pod opens, the new adult beetle flies away. This is a problem every year in our garden. Damage to siberian irises by iris weevils was also reported in seven of the fourteen gardens surveyed in this country and in one each in Belgium, England, and Germany. If the round entry hole in the wall of the pod can be located, inject a small amount of dimethoate through the hole to kill the pest. Indeed, if damage by the iris weevil is common, dimethoate can be injected into the pods of especially valuable crosses as a prophylactic measure.

Verbena bud moth (*Endothenia hebesana*): The verbena bud moth appears to be less of a problem than the iris weevil, as it was reported in only one Michigan garden. I have not been aware of it. The brownish gray moth, approximately 0.25 inch (6 millimeters) in length, lays its eggs on the seed pods; when the larvae emerge, they pierce the pod, enter it, and eat the seeds. Even the most painstaking search for these holes may prove futile, as they are very small and soon become invisible. The pupa develops inside the seed pod, and when the moth emerges from the pupa, it makes a larger hole and escapes, sometimes leaving the pupal casing in the hole.

I have found no means of controlling either the iris weevil or the verbena bud moth with certainty. Spraying the plant with dimethoate prior to blossom opening may kill the larvae in time to save some of the seeds, and although I have not tried it, perhaps one of the contact sprays will save the cross, if applied every few days for a few weeks after a cross is made. My own approach has been to make repeated crosses of especially prized parents. This has been successful, as the relative number of damaged pods has been small.

Miscellaneous Insect Pests

Cutworms: In most gardens surveyed, cutworms were a problem, especially in small seedlings, which they cut off just above ground level. Usually the seedling starts growth again but is, of course, set back. Juvenile parasitic nematodes kill cutworms and other grubs of that sort. If the number of seedlings is not too large, each can be protected by a "fence" of cardboard or plastic placed around it and pushed down into the soil. The central spools of paper towels and toilet tissue rolls, cut into 3-inch (7.5-centimeter) lengths, serve well for this purpose. For larger plantings a dusting of carbaryl along the seedling rows is very helpful. If a seedling is cut off by a cutworm, a search in the top few inches of soil around the plant will usually turn up the culprit before it damages other seedlings.

Spider mites (red) (*Tetranychus uricae*): Spider mites were reported as an occasionally severe problem in three of the gardens surveyed, all on the West Coast. In one it was noted that they particularly affected the 40-chromosome cultivars. Usually the damage to the leaves does not appear to hurt the plant seriously. Merely washing off the mites with the jet spray of the garden hose may be sufficient if infestation is mild (Witt 1993). For severe infestations, fluvalinate may be used.

Aphids: Aphids affected both 28- and 40-chromosome siberian irises in two of the gardens in this country, both on the West Coast, and in both gardens in England. Although aphids themselves cause relatively minor damage, they open the way to viral infection in tall bearded irises;

this may not be a problem in siberian irises since they appear not to be subject to the same viral diseases. Control aphids by spraying with malathion or other contact sprays; insecticidal soaps containing fatty acid salts are also useful. Among biological controls, ladybugs (*Hippodamia convergeus*), lacewings (*Chrysopacamea*), and aphid midges (*Aphidoletes aphidimyza*) are effective.

Thrips: Two species of thrips can damage irises. *Brematothrips iridis* attacks the leaves; as the leaves grow, the rasped areas come into view as discolored streaks and patches. Another species, most likely *Frankliniella tritici*, mars the flower's beauty with a characteristic rasping of developing petals. The damage thrips cause does not kill the plant but weakens it, hindering growth and reducing the number and size of flowers.

The leaf-damaging species is a common and severe problem in japanese irises but was reported in siberian irises in only one garden surveyed. In our own garden in Maine, almost every one of a thousand or more japanese irises will be affected unless the thrips are controlled, but the siberian irises growing nearby remain unaffected. The insects live for the most part in the lower halves of the leaves, where one leaf enfolds another, and hence these thrips are difficult to kill with contact pesticides unless applied heavily enough to infiltrate the enfolded leaves. For this reason a systemic pesticide such as dimethoate provides the best control; indeed, dimethoate applied against iris borers will take care of leaf-damaging thrips also. The species that attacks the flowers is controlled by dimethoate or by a contact pesticide.

Adult thrips are dark, antlike insects, barely visible to the naked eye but easily seen with a strong hand magnifier. Check for them by separating and inspecting the enfolded leaves. Since several generations of thrips emerge each year, slightly smaller, white, immature thrips are apt to be present also. If thrips have attacked siberian irises in your garden, spray a second time approximately ten days after the first application. Because of the repeated generations, a vigilant watch should be kept and the sprays repeated if thrips reappear.

Other Pests

Slugs and snails: Snails were judged a minor nuisance in only three of the gardens surveyed, one on the West Coast and the two in England, but slugs of various types were much more common, being present in most gardens, especially on the West Coast. The damage caused differs from place to place and year to year. Slugs can spoil flowers, but their real damage is to the leaves. In a severe infestation they can destroy a full row of small seedlings in a single night. They seek shelter from drying conditions under mulch or boards placed on the ground; check beneath such likely haunts periodically and kill the gathered slugs with a sprinkling of salt. Slug baits are very effective but must be placed with caution so that they cannot be eaten by pets. A common and useful measure is to set out shallow dishes filled with beer; slugs, attracted by the beer, fall in and drown. Pope (1988) has found that wood ashes scattered around the plant will repel slugs. Diatomaceous earth can be used in the same way.

Smaller animals: Mice, moles, voles, gophers, and the like, and even armadillos, do not directly attack irises as a rule but often damage rhizomes and roots in their search for grubs. Gophers may eat the roots of siberian irises (Abrego 1993), and voles overwintering under a straw mulch have been known to eat the rhizomes. Depending on conditions, moles can be merely an annoyance or a catastrophe (J. Hollingworth 1987, 1988). Means of control include poisoned baits and special traps made specifically for moles. None are very effective, however. For control of field mice, the garden cat is a great asset.

Larger animals: Rabbits, deer, and farm animals are among the larger animals that can cause damage. Rabbits may eat the leaves of small seedlings and also those of mature plants of some cultivars. The larger animals might chew the leaves of a few plants but cause damage mainly by walking through the bed. Materials claiming to be repellant to rabbits and deer are advertised, but I have had no occasion to use them and have heard conflicting opinions about them. Some friends are pleased with the results of hanging old nylon stockings stuffed with human hair and bars of strong soap among their plants to keep deer away, but others have been disappointed. So far as the large farm animals are concerned, the answer is to help your neighbors repair their fences.

The garden visitor: Fortunately, this is no longer the problem that it once was, although one still has rather bitter memories of the days when a camera fiend would take off a spent flower—ignoring the tag marking a cross—in order to have a better picture of the flower behind it, or the compulsively neat guest who would "help" the garden host by removing spent blooms. Visitors nowadays are usually aware of the rules of good garden manners, and modern attire will rarely wreak the havoc that billowing skirts once did. Still, dangling carryalls and camera equipment can be hazards, and one should not hesitate to ask that they not be taken into the garden rows if they are awkwardly oversized or are carelessly handled. If guests arrive in large numbers, it is well to limit walking between the rows as much as possible to avoid compacting the soil, especially if wet and of heavy type. Happily, the term "pest" scarcely remains appropriate for one's garden friends, whose visits add to the joys of gardening.

Chapter 7

Diseases

Although a few diseases and abnormalities of irises are nutritional or mechanical in nature, most are caused by infectious agents of microscopic and submicroscopic size, namely bacteria, viruses, fungi, and nematodes. Exact knowledge of the nature, prevalence, and control of the diseases affecting siberian irises does not exist in every case. The discussion in this chapter is based in part on my personal experience and study but especially on information provided by experienced growers worldwide who have generously shared their knowledge.

Diseases Due to Infectious Agents

Diseases caused by bacteria

Bacterial diseases are easily summarized. Two diseases, bacterial leaf blight (causative agent, *Xanthomonas tardicrescens*) and bacterial soft rot (causative agent, *Erwinia carotovora*) are serious problems in tall bearded irises but are not known in siberian irises. They had occurred in none of the eighteen gardens in our survey.

Diseases caused by viruses

Viral diseases require little comment. Several viral mosaic diseases occur in bearded and bulbous irises (Weiler 1978), and Barnett (1972)

71

suspects that all cultivars of those two groups may be infected with viruses but that most are resistant and show no evidence of disease. I know of no confirmed report of a viral disease in siberian irises.

Diseases caused by fungi

A formidable list of fungal diseases occur in bearded irises, namely botrytis rhizome rot, botrytis blossom blight, crown rot, root rot, fungal leaf spot, and rust. The first four are known to occur in siberian irises as well.

Botrytis rhizome rot (causative agent, *Sclerotinia [Botrytis] convoluta*): Prior to 1979 it was believed that botrytis rhizome rot occurred only in bearded irises, but in that year Robert Hollingworth (1979) identified it in siberian irises. Growers of siberian irises have since recognized this disease as a major—and widespread—problem. It was reported in both 28-and 40-chromosome siberian irises by most questionnaire respondents, including the four in Europe.

Features of the disease are characteristic and easily identified. The outermost leaves of the clump become brown, especially at their bases, and moist brown patches of rot spread through the leaves, which fall over at ground level. Occasionally, the rotted patches occur higher up in the leaves, which then droop over from that level. Gradually the leaves toward the center of the clump become affected also, but the outermost leaves are the first to show the disease. This is diagnostically important because in the other two disorders with browning of the leaves—damage by borers and scorch—the leaves first affected are those at the center of the clump. A careful search may reveal light gray collections of spores in the patches of rot at the base of the leaves.

Botrytis rhizome rot is favored by cool, wet conditions and therefore appears in the spring. If the disease is mild, the plant may recover without treatment as the weather becomes warmer and drier, but it is best to start treatment at once. Fortunately, this is simple and effective. A single heavy spray of benomyl or thiophanate-methyl at the rate of 1 table-spoon (15 milliliters) per gallon (3.8 liters) of water usually is sufficient. Use the solution to soak the soil close to the plant as well. If the disease has progressed to a more severe degree, spray a second time about ten days later. If the disease is serious, the plant can be lifted, washed, and soaked in the benomyl or thiophanate-methyl solution for half an hour and then replanted. The fungus appears to remain in the plant in a latent state and may reappear the next spring. Some cultivars appear to be more susceptible to botrytis rhizome rot than others. Any plant that shows susceptibility to the disease can be given the benomyl or thiophanate-methyl spray as a preventive measure each spring as growth starts. Unless that plant has some unusually important feature, it should not be used in hybridizing.

Botrytis blossom blight (causative agent, *Sclerotinia [Botrytis] cinerea*): Botrytis blossom blight was not listed as affecting siberian irises in the *Index of Plant Diseases in the United States* published by the United States Department of Agriculture (1960) but was reported to affect siberian as well as tall bearded irises in one of the gardens surveyed in Britain. It obviously is rare and does little damage except to the blossoms. It is controlled by spraying with benomyl or thiophanate-methyl used as for botrytis rhizome rot.

Crown rot (causative agent, *Sclerotium rolfsii*): Crown rot was listed by the United States Department of Agriculture (1960) as a fungal disease affecting siberian and other beardless irises in addition to the bearded irises. In our survey, crown rot was reported in a single southern California garden as affecting siberian irises, *Iris versicolor*, and japanese irises, in addition to the tall bearded irises, and was present in only tall bearded irises in two other gardens. It had previously occurred in a large planting of siberian irises in Michigan (R. M. Hollingworth 1985). In this particular and rather serious outbreak, benomyl and other fungicides had failed to control the disease. The garden area was reclaimed by destroying the diseased plants, fumigating the bed, and adding fresh soil. Siberian irises subsequently planted remained healthy, and there has been no recurrence of the disease (R. M. Hollingworth 1994).

Leaves of diseased plants turn yellow at their tops and rot at the base. In advanced disease, some rotting of the crown also occurs. A careful search will reveal the fungi in gray or tan cottony masses at the base of the leaves. The disease occurs in hot, moist weather in tall bearded irises in the southern United States.

Root rot: Several fungi—*Rhizoctonia solani, Fusarium, Pythium,* and *Phytophthora*—have been identified in the roots of tall bearded and bulbous irises stricken with root rot (Weiler 1978). In 1993 *Rhizoctonia, Phytophthora,* and *Fusarium* were isolated from both siberian and japanese irises that were diagnosed with scorch. This is detailed more fully in the discussion of scorch later in this chapter.

Diseases caused by nematodes

Nematodes are wormlike creatures too small to be seen with the naked eye but visible with the low-power lens of a microscope or even a powerful, double-lensed hand magnifier. Most of the some 15,000 described species of nematodes are harmless or even helpful creatures, living in soil or fresh or salt water, where they feed on fungi, bacteria, and algae. Some, however, are harmful to plants. Most of these live in the soil and merely nibble the roots from the outside. Others are endoparasites, that is, they live in the roots. The two species that affect irises, the root knot nematode and the meadow nematode, are endoparasitic.

Root knot nematode: A *Meloidogyne* species, the root knot nematode, appears to be the only nematode that causes serious damage to irises. Hager, one of the breeders who took part in our survey and who has studied the root knot problem very thoroughly, has found it seriously harmful in other irises but not in siberian irises. In the Belgian garden surveyed, however, root knot nematodes affected both 28- and 40-chromosome cultivars.

The characteristic pathologic changes are readily seen in the roots and consist of small nodules and a profusion of lateral, hairlike roots, which become intertwined and "knotted." The nodules are clearly visible to the naked eye. The active nematodes have the characteristic appearance of tiny worms, but in the cyst stage, in the nodules, they look like tiny pearls. Although the disease can be a serious problem in southern areas, it does not occur in the north, where the root knot nematode is apparently killed by winter cold.

In the past, control in bearded irises involved shaving off all roots at their attachment to the rhizome or immersing the rhizome and roots in water at 125 degrees Fahrenheit (51 degrees Celsius) for half an hour, but neither method has been practical for beardless irises. Fortunately, Hager (1987, 1992) has discovered that the disease can be controlled by treatment with dimethoate. The plant is lifted and washed, and dead roots are cut out. The plant is then soaked in dimethoate, 1 tablespoon (15 milliliters) per gallon (3.8 liters) of water (or as indicated in the manufacturer's directions) for one hour. Since the soil is also infested with the nematodes, it must be sterilized before the treated clump is replanted. This can be achieved by using nematicides, such as ethoprop and fenamiphos, or a nonselective soil fumigant, such as dazomet or metam-sodium. All are highly toxic and are restricted for use. Hager

(1992) reports that plants treated as described with dimethoate and re-planted in sterilized soil have remained free of the nematodes.

Meadow (or lesion) nematode (*Pratylenchus penetrans*): It is generally agreed that the meadow nematode is not a significant problem in siberian irises, but it appears to be ubiquitous, having been found without exception in the roots of irises of all types received in one year from various parts of the United States, England, Germany, Russia, and Japan (McEwen 1978a). Fortunately, the damage it causes is slight. In one study of mine, siberian irises were treated with ethoprop and planted in a bed sterilized with the soil fumigant metam-sodium. The same cultivars, untreated and planted in untreated soil, served as a control group. Over a three-year period the treated plants remained free of *Pratylenchus penetrans*. Their roots remained clear and normal compared with those of the untreated plants, which showed some brown streakings, but leaves, flowers, and growth were the same in both groups. By the end of three years, *Pratylenchus penetrans* began to reappear in the plants at the periphery of the treated bed, and in time would no doubt have invaded the entire bed. These results showed clearly that treated plants, free of the nematodes, would quickly become reinfested unless planted in sterilized soil. In view of the lack of evidence of any significant damage caused by the meadow nematode, however, I concluded from my study that treatment was unnecessary. These observations were made in Maine, and it is possible that the infestation can cause more pronounced symptoms under different conditions.

If one wishes to demonstrate *Pratylenchus penetrans*, it is easily done. Cut off a few small bits of roots, wash them, and place them in a small jar with a few drops of water. After a few hours, place a drop of the water on a glass slide and examine it with the low-power lens of a microscope. The wormlike nematodes are easily seen, thrashing about.

Disease of Uncertain Cause: Scorch

A disease for which a cause has not been proven can be accepted as an entity only on the basis of symptoms and physical features that are sufficiently characteristic to warrant such a conclusion. Scorch is such a disease, and its features are, indeed, characteristic. The leaves at the center of the clump begin to turn brown at their tips. The brown gradually spreads down to involve the whole leaf, but the leaves remain firmly attached to the rhizome. If the plant is lifted, the rhizome is found to be normally firm, but the roots are dead, with only the central stringlike part and the surrounding "skin" of the root remaining and the normally firm root tissue is gone. Another characteristic feature of scorch is that it tends not to spread to adjacent plants. Indeed, one can plant a new iris in exactly the same spot where a dying one has been removed without any sterilization of the soil, and the new plant remains healthy. These features have defined scorch in tall bearded irises, and it has been assumed that a disorder characterized by those same features in siberian and other beardless irises is the same disease.

These features are of great help in differential diagnosis. The facts that the leaves first affected are the central ones and remain firmly attached differentiate scorch from botrytis. With botrytis, the first leaves affected are the peripheral leaves, and they readily tear away. The central leaves are those first affected in borer damage also, but as in botrytis, they easily pull away, revealing soft, torn, and usually blackened ends.

Attempts to identify a causative agent have been inconclusive. Studies in the 1950s revealed nematodes "different" from those that cause root knot. In all probability, those nematodes were *Pratylenchus penetrans*, which species we now know is found in all types of irises without causing significant disease. In other studies at that time, various fungi — including *Fusarium*, *Pythium* and *Rhizoctonia* — were identified, but none were isolated consistently or exclusively, and attempts to reproduce the disease by inoculating healthy bearded irises with those fungi were unsuccessful (Dimock 1959).

Bald (1969) believed that a *Pseudomonas* was responsible for scorch in bearded irises, but Wadekamper (1972) was unable to confirm this — and failed to identify any other microorganism as the culprit. Hence scorch continued to be considered a disease of unknown cause until 1988, when electronmicroscopic studies revealed mycoplasma-like organisms (MLOs) in tall bearded irises diagnosed with the affliction (Sjolund et al 1990). MLOs are similar to bacteria but lack cell walls. In Sjolund's studies, they were found to be blocking the nutritive channels of the plants, resulting in death by starvation.

Sjolund's electronmicroscopic pictures are convincing, and the implication of MLOs as the cause of scorch is very attractive as it would explain the failure of the disease to spread to adjacent plants. Other plants in the garden with features of scorch are few and widely scattered; this fits the pattern of diseases caused by MLOs, which microorganisms can live only in living tissue and hence cannot spread directly from one plant to another across open space or soil. Instead they depend upon insect vectors for transmission. When the vector feeds upon a sick plant, the MLOs enter its tissue and are carried by the vector to another host plant. This remains a convincing cause of scorch in tall bearded irises, but for three consecutive years, siberian and japanese irises diagnosed with what I prefer to think of as the scorchlike syndrome were studied electronmicroscopically, and no evidence of MLOs was found (Sjolund 1993).

Although scorchlike syndrome is nearly always fatal to the affected plant, it has not been a serious cause of concern because so few plants in any one area are stricken—perhaps two or three, widely scattered, in a planting of many hundreds. But in 1992 the situation changed: a severe outbreak of what was thought to be scorch occurred in a nursery in Germany, coinciding with an apparent increase in the disease in the United States. In response to mounting concern, the American Iris Society is sponsoring a broad, long-term study of scorch, attempting to discover its cause and prevalence, as well as possible means of cure. The project will be carried out over several growing seasons; results are pending, but early findings point to several fungi as possible causative agents.

Fortunately the devastating outbreak in the nursery in Germany, which struck irises of all types, appears to have been brought under control. The larvae of flea beetles are known to destroy the roots of many plants, and laboratory studies at the nursery in Germany revealed a species of flea beetle (*Aphthona nonstriata*, also known as *A. coerulea*) in the roots of the affected plants. Two insecticides effective against flea beetles were therefore applied at once, and annually since. The number of diseased plants decreased rapidly, and the incidence of scorch has returned to the levels of previous decades, with only an occasional affected plant among hundreds of healthy siberian and japanese irises.

Flea beetles have not been linked with scorchlike syndrome in siberian and japanese irises in the United States. Rather, every plant studied in two fairly severe outbreaks of the disease, as well as in the usual, infrequent examples of scorch in large plantings, has been found to have the fungus *Rhizoctonia* in the roots, often associated with *Fusarium*, *Pythium*, or *Phytophthora*—the same four fungi mentioned earlier as having been found in tall bearded and bulbous irises with root rot. Whereas there can be no doubt that these fungi are present in the diseased plants, it is not yet known whether they are the primary cause or are merely playing a secondary role.

Thus, the cause of scorchlike syndrome has been attributed variously to MLOs in tall bearded irises, to flea beetles in irises of all types in the European outbreaks, and to certain fungi in siberian and japanese irises in the United States. Research continues but results to date suggest that what has been called scorch—at least in siberian and japanese irises—is not a disease with a single cause but rather a syndrome that results from several different causes. Current evidence supports the view that the scorchlike syndrome can be caused by any infectious agent—or, possibly, mechanical or nutritional abnormality—that destroys the roots without apparent harm to the rhizome or crown.

Treatment of the diseased plants necessarily depends on the cause. If flea beetles are found in the roots, an insecticide (such as fenvalerate, fluvalinate, or permethrin) would be indicated. Tall bearded irises infested with MLOs have been successfully treated by heating the rhizome at 104 degrees Fahrenheit (40 degrees Celsius) for three or four days, or with soil drenches of the antibiotics tetracycline or streptomycin (Sjolund et al 1990). Finally, if the aforementioned fungi are present, a combined spray of thiophanate methyl (for *Rhizoctonia* and *Fusarium*) and metalaxyl (for *Pythium* and *Phytophthora*) can be recommended on a trial basis for prevention and, one may hope, for cure.

Since the early 1980s, many studies have been conducted on the effect of various composts on pathogenic fungi in the soil, including the four associated with the scorchlike syndrome. Composts prepared from spruce and hemlock bark inoculated with biocontrol agents such as *Trichoderma* and *Flavobacterium* species have been shown to suppress diseases caused by these fungi. The conditions governing the efficacy of the biological control agents must be strictly monitored, however, and more testing is needed before composts fortified with biocontrol agents become available for practical garden use (Hoitink and Grebus 1994).

Diseases Due to Nutritional and Mechanical Causes

Nutritional deficiencies

Normal garden loam is so well supplied with all the necessary nutritional elements that siberian irises planted in a newly made garden bed will grow quite well for several years without fertilizer. In time, however, plants in such a bed will deteriorate unless they are fed. Within the broad range of possible nutritional deficiencies, two with the similar symptom of yellowing leaves require individual consideration. The yellowing of the leaves is known as chlorosis, from the Greek *chlöros*, meaning yellowish green. At least twelve causes of chlorosis are known (Korcak 1987), but the two principal ones are due to nitrogen and iron deficiencies.

Nitrogen deficiency chlorosis can be considered very briefly. The entire leaf of the affected plant turns yellowish, including the veins. Treatment consists of an application of high nitrogen fertilizer, using a soluble fertilizer for its quick effect plus a granular fertilizer for its more lasting action.

Iron deficiency chlorosis is distinguished from nitrogen deficiency chlorosis by close examination of the leaves. Although the leaves of affected plants turn yellow, the veins remain green, unless the disease is very advanced. Iron is essential for the action of chlorophyll in photosynthesis, the process by which the sun's energy is utilized for the survival and growth of all green plants. In extremely rare instances, chlorosis may be due to an actual lack of iron in the soil, but the usual cause is an inability of the plant to utilize iron that is present in the soil in ample amounts but in insoluble form. Solubility decreases as the pH of the soil increases. Phosphates in the soil in too high amounts can also lead to iron deficiency chlorosis by combining with the iron to form insoluble iron phosphate. For this reason superphosphate fertilizers (0–46–0) must be used with caution for surface application.

Calcium is one of the elements needed by plants, but in excessive amounts it can be harmful and cause iron deficiency chlorosis indirectly. Calcium is in the soil as calcium carbonate, derived largely from limestone. In large amounts the carbonate can be harmful by raising the soil pH to alkaline levels, which increases the insolubility of the available iron. Whether excess calcium can contribute to chlorosis in other ways has been questioned, but recent studies support the view that it does not (Korcak 1992).

The first step in treating chlorosis due to iron deficiency is to spray the plant with iron chelate according to the manufacturer's directions. Iron chelate quickly corrects the lack of iron available to the plant because it is absorbed by the plant directly, but it does not affect the pH, and its benefit will be temporary unless the pH is lowered. For this purpose, iron in the form of ferrous sulfate is excellent as it lowers the pH and also provides iron in a more lasting—although not immediately available—form. The combined use of iron chelate and ferrous sulfate is recommended.

The appearance of iron deficiency chlorosis in a few plants is a warning that the whole bed requires iron. In such a situation, ferrous sulfate can be used for the whole bed as a preventive measure, but iron chelate, with its quickly curative action, need be applied only to the plants that are already chlorotic.

Mechanically induced abnormality

Accordion pleating of leaves is not a symptom of disease but merely a mechanically induced disarrangement of leaf growth. Leaves with this abnormality show a short area of back-and-forth folding, like accordion pleating, although the rest of the leaf is smooth. The central leaves, which are the ones that grow fastest, are especially apt to be affected. A plant that exhibits the abnormality one year is no more likely than any other to show it the next. The most probable explanation of accordion pleating is that it is the result of a temporary check in the leaf's ability to become longer. The leaves enfold each other toward the base of the plant; normally as a leaf grows longer, it slips by the enfolding ones. If for some reason, such as loss of lubrication or an obstruction, the leaf cannot move upward, growth continues nevertheless and the leaf folds back and forth tightly within the leaves that enfold it. When conditions change, permitting upward movement once again, the leaf elongates as usual, showing accordion pleating between smooth, unaffected portions.

In summary, siberian irises of both the 28- and 40-chromosome groups are remarkably free of serious diseases. Botrytis root rot is the most frequent problem but can be controlled. Damage by the root knot nematode is limited to southern areas and successful means of cure are now known. A scorchlike syndrome in siberian irises remains of uncertain cause but except in rare instances it is a quantitatively small problem and ongoing studies suggest that knowledge of cause and means of control may be at hand.

Chapter 8

Hybridizing

Hybridizing is the process of placing the pollen of one species or cultivar on the stigma of another in order to obtain seeds—and eventually plants—containing genes from both parents. The resulting plants are hybrids. At first the term "hybrid" referred strictly to a plant that resulted from a cross of two different species. Over the years, however, its meaning has been broadened to include any seedling in which the genes have been mixed, and thus, by this last definition, even seedlings that result from selfing a flower with its own pollen are hybrids. The ranks of those who make crosses encompass a wide range, from the many who casually cross an occasional flower to the seriously dedicated hybridizer. All serious hybridizers love their gardens, but their chief interest is not the beautiful flowers around them but the still more beautiful ones that do not yet exist.

Planned vs natural crosses

In the late 1800s and early 1900s, when interest in siberian irises changed from collecting new species to obtaining new, improved cultivars, all the seeds planted came from natural crosses made by insects. New seedlings from such natural crosses are still introduced each year. Some of the most valued cultivars owe their origin to natural crosses, including 'White Swirl', which is perhaps the most important siberian iris ever introduced. For all its significance, however, it came about in a most inefficient way. There was a rather widely accepted idea at the time that it was useless to try to make controlled crosses with siberian irises because they were believed to cross with their own pollen even before the bud opened. Fred Cassebeer, in whose garden 'White Swirl' originated, believed this erroneous concept and therefore did not make planned crosses with siberian irises as he did with his tall bearded irises. He told me that he collected a full bushel basket of naturally occurring pods in his large planting of siberian irises. From the thousands of resulting seedlings came 'White Swirl'.

Neither parent is known in most of Cassebeer's seedlings, which is unusual. More commonly in natural crosses, the pod parent is known, for the iris growers observe pods forming on cultivars they particularly like and plant the resulting seeds. The introducer of such a new seedling may be pleased with it but lacks the satisfaction of having played any very active role in its creation and, of course, knows only the pod parent.

The alternative is the planned, protected cross. Isabella Preston was, in the 1930s, one of the first to make mostly planned crosses and that practice was greatly encouraged by McGarvey (1975). Both parents of the majority of new introductions are now known, a trend that has occurred for two principal reasons. The first is the greater efficiency of the method, and the second is the obvious advantage of being able to record the full genetic background of the plant.

Goals

Once the decision has been made to take up hybridizing in a serious way, the beginner had best settle upon goals toward which to work. It is natural simply to start crossing pretty flowers and, indeed, this can provide lovely new seedlings, but very probably, few will be enough better than the parents or other cultivars in commerce to warrant introduction. The end results are still less worthwhile if one starts with inferior parents, as the neophyte all too often does. Clearly, one is not likely to produce the flower of the future by starting with cultivars long since outdated, except when their use is indicated by a particular hybridizing goal. By all means, define goals and then start with the best parents to reach those goals.

A primary decision is whether to work with the 28- or 40-chromosome cultivars, or both. Relatively few hybridizers are working with the 40-chromosome group, so it is perhaps a more open field for the beginner. On the other hand, cultivars of that group are less easy to grow in regions that are very cold or dry.

The selection of goals is naturally a matter of personal choice, but here are some possibilities:

- new colors, such as green, orange, and brown;
- new color combinations and patterns;
- improved colors, to obtain spectrum reds and blues and true pinks, unmixed with lavender;
- improved features, such as ruffling, crimped edges, feathered midribs, and wide, tufted styles;
- improved branching and bud count;
- improved resistance to pests and diseases;
- miniatures with short stalks bearing flowers of proportionately small size;
- early, late, and—especially—repeat bloomers, to extend the season;
- adaptability to unfavorable conditions, to extend the growing range;
- vigorous plants and handsome foliage;
- fragrance.

Discussion of floral forms needs special attention. Hybridizers were so attracted to the lovely round, flaring form and wide falls of 'White Swirl' that it was chosen again and again as a parent, and most cultivars introduced since 1960 show its influence. There can be no question that this new form is a most valuable advance in siberian irises. Unfortunately, cultivars with the traditional form of gracefully arched, more narrow falls have tended to be neglected by hybridizers. Renewed efforts with these more traditional forms is yet another important hybridizing goal. Not only are they beautiful in their own right but they also provide lovely contrast for the flowers descended from 'White Swirl'. I am continually impressed by the way in which the more traditional flowers— 'Chartreuse Bounty', 'Soft Blue', and 'Shaker's Prayer', for example— when intermixed with the big, round tetraploids, enhance the beauty and interest of our entire display bed.

Approaches

Having settled on certain goals, the hybrizider's next question is to consider the various types of breeding approaches that may be used to achieve them. The inefficiency and limitations of harvesting seeds from natural crosses made by insects have been pointed out. A better approach is the planned cross, which is of three general types: selfing, outcrossing, and line breeding.

"Selfing" is the term used for fertilizing a cultivar with its own pollen. It can be used in the hope of exaggerating some promising genetic feature in that plant but is of limited value in developing new features. Outcrossing and line breeding are the hybridizer's basic tools.

Outcrossing is the practice of selecting unrelated cultivars for a cross. An extreme example of outcrossing is the crossing of different species, such as the interspecies crossing of *Iris sibirica* and *I. sanguinea* in the 1930s and '40s, which led to the modern siberian iris hybrids. More recently, outcrossing focuses on plants from different genetic breeding lines, crossed in the hope of introducing new features in seedlings. Even more commonly, the hybridizer is unconcerned with the background parentage of the cultivars selected for crossing but instead selects plants that on the basis of their appearance give promise of developing some particular goal.

Once the hybridizer has developed seedlings of real merit, with distinctive, desirable features, the time has come to turn to line breeding, crossing related seedlings to establish a personal breeding line. This can involve crossing a seedling with one of its parents (backcrossing) or with siblings or less closely related relatives. The hybridizer must, however, be alert to the continued usefulness of outcrossing, which approach should be revisited from time to time to introduce some new, desired feature and, perhaps, to maintain hybrid vigor.

Basic principles

The reproductive organs of the siberian iris flower—the anthers, styles, stigmas, and ovary—are illustrated in Figures 4-1 and 8-1; in Figure 8-1, all standards, falls, and spathes have been removed the better to reveal the reproductive features. The female reproductive organ, or pistil, consists of the ovary, styles, and stigmas. The ovary is made up of three longitudinal compartments, each one of which extends upward to one of the three styles. Each style ends near its top in a stigma; the function of each stigma is to receive the pollen. The ovary contains the ovules, which in turn contain the egg cells. After fertilization, these develop into the seeds. The male organ is the stamen, consisting of a pollen-bearing anther held at the end of a slender filament.

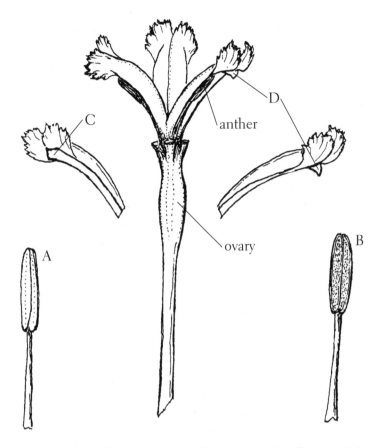

Figure 8-1. The reproductive organs of a siberian iris flower: A) immature anther, not yet dehisced; B) mature, dehisced anther, dotted with
pollen; C) style's underside, with an immature stigma tightly closed
against it; and D) mature stigmas, opened and ready for crossing.

The falls and standards serve to support and protect the reproductive
organs and perhaps, through their colors, to attract nectar-seeking bees.
The bees land at the base of the falls at the signal area and then work
their large, hairy bodies down between the falls and styles to reach the
nectar at their juncture. As seen in Figure 8-1, the anthers are just under
the styles and very close to the stigmas. After a flower opens, the anthers
mature and open (dehisce), exposing their pollen; the stigmas mature
and open shortly thereafter. Hence it is inevitable that as the bee works

its way down between style and fall, it will brush against both the stigma and anther, fertilizing the flower with either its own pollen or with pollen from the last visited flower.

The basic principle in making a planned cross is obvious and very simple—yet absolutely essential: the hybridizer must make the cross before the bud has opened spontaneously and must protect all flowers selected to be parents from foraging insects. If the cross is made after the flower has opened, the hybridizer can be sure of only the pod parent of resulting seedlings. The pollen parent may not be the one used by the hybridizer but rather some unknown parent whose pollen was carried by a bee before the cross was made; the bee may have either selfed the flower or brought the pollen from another plant. Some natural protection against selfing is in place: the anther matures some hours earlier than the stigma, and thus the pollen may be largely dispersed by the time the stigma opens.

The biological process of fertilization is remarkable. Almost immediately after the pollen grains are deposited on the stigma, a microscopically narrow tubule starts to grow from each pollen grain down through the style to the ovary, a distance of 1.5 inches (3.5 centimeters) or more. This is accomplished in a few hours. In the ovary a nucleus on the tubule fuses with an egg cell in the ovule and fertilization occurs. Within a week one can judge whether the cross has been successful for, if it has, the ovary begins to grow larger and forms a seed pod. By the end of two and a half to three months, the capsule is mature and filled with seeds, each one of which came from a single egg cell fertilized by a single pollen grain.

Methods

The basic rule of hybridizing siberian irises is to make the cross before the bud has opened naturally. All the various methods employed by hybridizers thus begin in the same manner: the bud is opened by hand and the anthers removed, to prevent self-pollination. In some the cross is made at once with pollen collected for the purpose; in others the flower is protected in such a way that insects cannot gain entrance, and the cross is made later when pollen and stigma are fully mature. A colleague and I carried out a series of trials to determine how mature pollen and stigma must be for a successful cross (McEwen and Warburton 1971). Immature pollen and stigmas were those in buds not expected to open naturally for another twelve hours or more. Mature stigmas and pollen were defined as those in balloon-stage buds expected to open in another hour or two; stigmas and pollen are not fully mature at that time but are approaching maturity. As might be expected, crosses made with either immature stigmas or immature pollen—or both—were not often successful (14 to 23 percent successful), whereas much greater success was achieved when both stigmas and pollen were approaching maturity (72 to 79 percent successful).

In the 1950s, the importance of making planned crosses and also the need to protect the flower from foraging bees first became appreciated. The buds of plants selected to be parents were gently opened by hand, anthers were removed, the cross was made, and the flower was then protected by "bagging" it, that is, by tying a paper bag or piece of cheesecloth or other light cloth over it. McGarvey later modified this by omitting the bagging and instead lifted the falls up after the cross had been made and tied them at the top. His purpose, in addition to protecting the flower, was to keep the pollen and stigmas cool and fresh while they finished maturing. In the aforementioned study, McGarvey's new method of tying up the falls proved better than the traditional method of bagging the flowers, resulting in distinctly more successful crosses (McEwen and Warburton 1971). One other trial in the study is worth mention. In it, twenty buds opened at balloon stage had the standards, falls, and anthers removed and were left unprotected. Even with the stigmas left open to the bees, not one set a pod.

Hybridizers use various methods to achieve a cross; my three preferences are as follows. With method one, balloon-stage buds of the two selected parents are gently opened by hand, and standards and stamens are carefully removed with forceps. The stamens are placed—anther end down—in the cuplike space formed by the styles, where they are conveniently stored until needed. The falls are then raised and tied with a piece of the plant's leaf or a twist tie. Next day the flowers are again opened, the reciprocal crosses are made, and the falls are again tied up. This method has proved very successful and is quite satisfactory if one has only a few crosses to make, but if one has many flowers prepared for crossing, widely distributed in a large hybridizing garden, remembering and finding those flowers the next day, or even later the same day, can be time-consuming and frustrating.

Method two is the same as method one except that the crosses are made at once. Even though the blossom will open naturally in another hour, the anthers will at best be only partly dehisced, and the stigmas will still be closed against the styles. Using a wooden toothpick along the anther's line of opening will expose the pollen. The toothpick can then be gently used to lift open the stigma of the other parent flower and to spread pollen on it. The falls are then brought up and tied.

Method three works on the assumption that flowers with standards, falls, and anthers removed—and only the styles left—can be expected to remain unfertilized even though the stigmas are not protected. Such a flower is crossed with the aid of a toothpick as in method two and that is all there is to it. Schafer (1989) reports a success rate of 85 percent, which is at least as high as mine using methods one and two. I had assumed that the flowers with only the styles left in place remained unfertilized because the bees were not attracted to them and perhaps did not recognize them as flowers, but this is not the case. In recent years I have used this method almost exclusively and have been surprised at the frequency with which the bees go to these dismembered flowers. Indeed, they seem to prefer them, perhaps because some attractant is made more apparent to them. Certainly it is easier for the bees to have the nectar laid open for them than to have to work their way down between fall and style to reach it. I have watched many bees come to these flowers, but in no instance did their bodies touch a stigma as there was nothing to prevent them from flying directly to the nectary at the juncture of fall and style.

To test the reliability of method three, a simple experiment was carried out. Approximately 100 buds of japanese irises were allowed to open in the normal fashion. A similar group of buds was opened by hand, and falls, standards, and anthers were removed. Pods were set on 46 percent of the normal flowers but on only 2 percent of those with falls, standards, and anthers removed. I conclude from these results that although method three is not 100 percent safe, it is very nearly so, and I believe similar results can be expected with siberian irises. Indeed, our small-scale experiment (McEwen and Warburton 1971) and the larger trials by Schafer (1989) bear this out.

Whatever method is used, the tag identifying the cross must be fastened on as soon as the cross is made. Many hybridizers attach small cardboard tags with string. This is satisfactory in some gardens, but in areas subject to rain accompanied by high winds, plastic tags fastened with light wire are much safer and are very easy to use. Fasten the tag below the ovary, where it will identify the pod as it develops.

Crosses are much more likely to be successful when it is cool and moist than when it is hot and dry. They are rarely successful on very hot days. Since the entire process from pollination to fertilization takes only a few hours, a subsequent rain should not spoil the cross. If rain threatens soon, protect the cross with a "raincoat." Place a plastic sandwich bag over the flower and tie it around the stem. Be sure to tear off the fold of a fold-lock sandwich bag; otherwise it fills with water and can become heavy enough to break off the flower.

All hybridizers have their own system of record keeping. At a minimum, the serial number of the cross should be written on the tag corresponding with the number of the cross entered in the record book, commonly referred to as the stud book. One should also record the date and the names or seedling numbers of the two parents, writing the pod parent first.

Whether they are the result of planned or of natural crosses, pods wanted for their seeds must be watched and harvested before they can open and spill their precious cargo. If the hybridizer must be away at this critical time, a loose netting can be tied around the pod in advance to catch seeds as they fall, or the pod can be harvested if reasonably close to maturity. The subject of seed harvest is taken up in more detail in Chapter 10.

Pollen storage

In the three methods of making crosses just described, the pollen involved has been freshly obtained at the time of the cross. Often, however, the hybridizer wishes to use as the pollen parent a plant that will have finished blooming before the desired pod parent starts, or one from a friend's garden, a great distance away. One can then choose the best storage method from a variety of options, depending on the length of time the pollen is to be kept.

If it is to be stored only a day or two, the pollen can be scraped off the anther into a folded square of waxed paper and placed in a screwtop jar. Refrigerate the jar at temperatures above freezing and make sure that no moisture can get into it. If storage is to be for several weeks, add 1 teaspoon (5 milliliters) or more of a drying agent, such as silica gel or anhydrous calcium chloride, to the jar along with the pollen. The small paper or capsule-like packets that pharmaceutical companies place in medicine containers before shipping make very convenient drying agents; the pharmacist discards these and will provide them without charge. As a rule of thumb, the packets should fill approximately one quarter of the jar's volume.

Pollen placed in a tightly sealed screwtop jar and stored in the freezing compartment of the refrigerator remains effective for several months. Still longer storage, as from one season to the next, requires more elaborate laboratory equipment than the average gardener has. If frozen and dried at high vacuum in hermetically sealed glass vials, pollen can remain effective for years.

Genetic notes

This book is not the place for a detailed discussion of genetic rules and principles affecting hybridizing, but the novice should be aware of several practical considerations. The violet-blue color of siberian irises of the 28-chromosome group is genetically dominant, as would be expected of the predominant color of the species. Both white and the wine-red typical of the "red" siberian irises are recessive to blue. If one crosses a blue with a white, all the resulting seedlings will be blue, but if one of those seedlings is selfed or crossed with siblings, blue and white progeny will result in the ratio of roughly three to one, blues to whites, in accordance with Mendelian laws. Often, crossing two blue cultivars yields some white seedlings. In the same way, crossing the recessive wine-red color with the dominant blue results in all blues in the first generation and roughly three blues to one red in the next.

Crossing reds and whites also usually results in only blue seedlings in the first generation, with segregation into white, blue, and red in approximately Mendelian ratios in the second. Although only blues are expected in the first generation, the blue often has a reddish tinge and a few light reds can also occur. Crosses of pinks with whites give similar results.

Trials by Tiffney (1971) indicate that results of crossing white siberian irises with other whites depends on the background of the parents. Albino forms of *Iris sanguinea* are a lovely pure white, whereas the rarer albino forms of *I. sibirica* are a less pure white, with some bluish gray tones at the base of the falls. Crossing the *I. sanguinea* type white with modern white siberian irises resulted in only white, but crossing 'White Swirl', 'Snowcrest', and 'Snow Queen' with an albino *I. sibirica* resulted in only medium to light blue seedlings. Further crossing of these same first-generation seedlings led to some white and some blue flowers (Tiffney 1971).

These results suggest that *Iris sanguinea* predominates in the background of most modern white siberian irises. Supporting this view is the lovely color and form of 'Snow Queen', the collected cultivar of *I. sanguinea* that made such an impression when it was brought to the West from Japan in 1900. Surely the popularity of 'Snow Queen' in the early decades of this century led to its prevailing use as a white parent, just as the outstanding features of 'White Swirl' did fifty years later.

Developments for the future

The extraordinary achievements made possible by the new techniques of genetic engineering, including gene transfer, are widely appreciated (Smith 1993; Zimmermann 1994). In their application to plants, these high-tech scientific methods are very different from those of traditional hybridizing, but the two have in common the purpose of changing and, one hopes, improving upon what has occurred in nature. The hybridizer hopes to reach certain goals—such as the development of a spectrum red siberian iris—by combining and recombining genes of promising parent plants by crossing them. Unless some lucky break occurs, as happened with the color yellow (McEwen 1987), this process takes many generations, if indeed it can be accomplished at all. In genetic engineering, the gene or genes that will produce the true red color can, at least theoretically, be obtained from a donor plant that could not be used in a traditional cross and inserted into the host plant in a single generation.

Naturally, first efforts have been directed toward food plants; the techniques of gene transfer are bringing about desirable changes in cereals, vegetables, and other food plants that would have taken hundreds of years using ordinary hybridizing methods. But some experiments have already been carried out with ornamentals (Meyer et al 1987). The possibilities are many—true colors and new colors; repeat bloom and rebloom; fragrance; built-in resistance to diseases and pests; ability to withstand drought, cold, or adverse conditions of various kinds—but the methods are extremely complex. First the particular gene or genes that control the desired trait must be identified. Next one must find those complete genes among the thousands of genes in the donor plant. That gene must then be "cut" from the DNA molecule of the donor plant in such a way that it can permanently attach itself into the new recipient DNA molecule. This gene is then cloned into a plasmid or virus, which allows the gene to replicate and, if the carrier is suitable, permits the gene to be transferred from donor to recipient. The carrier of the gene into the new cell is called the vector. A common vector is the Ti plasmid of the bacterium *Agromycetum tumificiens*, which causes crown gall in certain plants. This plasmid is capable of carrying the desired donor DNA into some host plants but is ineffective with monocot plants and thus cannot be expected to succeed with irises. Just developing a suitable vector for siberian irises could be a major challenge. One method involves coating minute tungsten or gold pellets with the desired gene or genes and "shooting" them into the cells of the recipient plant by means of a "gun" powered with high-pressure gas.

The procedures that result in the identification, isolation, and cloning of genes and their introduction into new plants are very expensive and time-consuming, requiring complex laboratory technology. Although it is conceptually possible, for example, to introduce petunia red into a siberian iris using genetic engineering, it is not yet economically feasible. As the technology is simplified, it is likely that such experiments can and will be done. These dramatic new developments will require years to be achieved in irises, but that they can eventually be achieved appears to be certain.

Active hybridizers

The following list of serious, contemporary hybridizers of siberian irises in the United States is no doubt incomplete, and I apologize to all I have missed. Hybridizers in other countries are discussed in Chapter 14.

Terry Aitken
608 NW 119th Street
Vancouver, Washington 98685

Dana Borglum
2202 Austin Road
Geneva, New York 14456

Louise Bellagamba
11431 Old Saint Charles Road
Bridgeton, Missouri 63044-3075

George C. Bush
1739 Memory Lane Extd
York, Pennsylvania 17402

Robert Bauer and John Coble
9823 East Michigan Avenue
Galesburg, Michigan 49053

Arthur Cronin
10, 920 Oakwood Road
Roscommon, Michigan
    48653-0024

James L. Ennenga
1621 North 85th Street
Omaha, Nebraska 68114

Chandler Fulton
21 Hillcrest Road
Weston, Massachusetts
    02193-2020

Dale Hamblin
152 North Idlewild
Mundelein, Illinois 60060

Calvin Helsley
P.O. Box 306
Mansfield, Missouri 65704

Robert Hollingworth
124 Sherwood Road East
Williamston, Michigan 48895

Sterling Innerst
2700-A Oakland Road
Dover, Pennsylvania 17315

Harry B. Kuesel
4 Larkdale Drive
Littleton, Colorado 80123

Carla M. Lankow
11118 169th Avenue SE
Renton, Washington 98056

Clarence Mahan
7311 Churchill Road
McLean, Virginia 22101

Currier McEwen
RR1, Box 818
South Harpswell, Maine
    04079

Anna Mae Miller
6065 North 16th Street
Kalamazoo, Michigan 49007

Kevin J. Morley
8404 Cherry
Kansas City, Missouri 64131

Shirley L. Pope
39 Highland Avenue
Gorham, Maine
    04038-1701

Lorena M. Reid
41886 McKenzie Highway
Springfield, Oregon 97478

Martin Schafer
337 Acton Street
Carlisle, Massachusetts 01741

Nancy and David Silverberg
32009 South Ona Way
Molalla, Oregon 97038

Harold L. Stahly
8343 Manchester Drive
Grand Blanc, Michigan 48439

John W. White
193 Jackson Hill Road
Minot, Maine 04258

Steve Varner
Route 3, Box 5
Monticello, Illinois 61856

Sharon Hayes Whitney
RR1, Box 847
South Harpswell, Maine 04079

Julius Wadekamper
15980 Canby Avenue
Faribault, Minnesota 55021

Jean G. Witt
16516 25th NE
Seattle, Washington 98155

Kenneth Waite
6 Tow Path Lane
Westfield, Massachusetts
    01085-4532

John W. Wood
2654 Prospect Church Road
Mooresboro, North Carolina
    28114

Chapter 9

Wide-Cross Hybrids

Wide-cross hybrids are seedlings resulting from interseries and inter-species crosses. The "Check List of Iris Species Hybrids" in Appendix C of *Garden Irises* (Heinig 1959) records the then-known wide-cross hybrids involving siberian irises. Of the interseries hybrids listed, the largest number were with series *Californicae*. Of these, twenty-four were from crosses with siberian irises of the 40-chromosome group but only four were with species of the 28-chromosome group. In addition, there were three crosses of 40-chromosome species with *Iris tenax*, two of 40-chromosome species with louisiana irises, and two of 28-chromosome species with *I. setosa*. One each was recorded of 40-chromosome species with *I. bracteata*, *I. chrysophylla*, *I. grant-duffii*, *I. hartwegii*, *I. laevigata*, and *I. longipetala*; one each was recorded of 28-chromosome species with *I. laevigata*, *I. longipetala*, *I. pseudacorus*, *I. versicolor*, and *I. virginica*. Eleven hybrids were listed from crosses between the two subseries of series *Sibiricae*. Interestingly, only seventeen crosses between species of the 40-chromosome siberian irises were given, and only two between *I. sibirica* and *I. sanguinea*—undoubtedly because at the time, hybrids between these last two species were so taken for granted and so numerous that it was considered unnecessary to list them. Of course there have been many, many more. It is likely that few modern 40-chromosome cultivars go back to a single species, and perhaps no modern 28-chromosome cultivar does not have genes from both *I. sibirica* and *I. sanguinea*.

Even this brief summary of the "Check List of Iris Species Hybrids" reveals a great deal about which attempted crosses were successful. It reflects not only the interest that early hybridizers had in using particular species but also that some species crossed readily, whereas others did not.

All hybridizers know that crosses between members of the same species are relatively easy and can be expected to give seedlings that are fertile, but crosses between members of widely different species and series can be another matter. Some, such as two species of subseries *Sibiricae* (*Iris sibirica* and *I. sanguinea*), cross readily, yielding fertile seedlings, as do crosses between all species of subseries *Chrysographes*. In contrast, crosses between these two subseries are rarely successful, and when they do succeed the resulting seedlings are sterile. The one exception I am aware of is William McGarvey's 'Foretell', which is fertile with members of subseries *Sibiricae*. All seedlings I have obtained using 'Foretell' as a parent have, in turn, been sterile, however. The species of series *Californicae* also cross quite readily. Some interseries crosses are quite easy, for example, those between the *Californicae* and the siberian irises of subseries *Chrysographes*. This cross produces the interseries hybrids customarily referred to as Calsibes.

On the other hand, many interspecies crosses are very difficult, and most interseries crosses fail. In general, one may assume that the more similar biologically the two prospective parents are, the more likely they are to cross successfully. For example, both the 40-chromosome siberian irises and the species of the *Californicae* have forty chromosomes, and thus they cross readily. In contrast, crosses of the 28-chromosome siberian irises and the 40-chromosome *Californicae* rarely succeed.

A further problem is that even when wide-cross hybrids are achieved—as with the Calsibes—lovely as they may be, they cannot in turn be used as parents because they are sterile. The reasons for this are explained by the genetic mechanisms involved, and hence a brief review of these mechanisms may be helpful.

Reproduction in plants is of two types: vegetative and sexual. Vegetative reproduction is the natural growth of the plant. As the clump enlarges, it can be separated into small individual fans, each of which is biologically and genetically identical to the original. This growth occurs through division of the somatic (body) cells of the plant. It is essential that the two daughter cells resulting from the division have the same number of chromosomes as the cell from which they came. This is accomplished by a process known as mitosis. During mitosis, the chromosomes gather in a somewhat disclike arrangement at the center of the cell and divide, and the two sets move to opposite sides of the cell. Hence when the cell divides, the two new cells have the same number of chromosomes as the cell from which they came.

Sexual reproduction demands a very different process, that of reduction division. The two sets of chromosomes normally present in diploid somatic cells are reduced to single sets in the reproductive cells: the pollen and the eggs. Thus when the two reproductive cells fuse at fertilization, the cells of the resulting embryo have the numbers of chromosomes characteristic of that species. This process of reduction division is known as meiosis. The process starts with steps similar to those of mitosis, with the chromosomes lining up at the center of the cell. Instead of dividing, however, the like chromosomes line up next to each other and one set moves to one side of the cell and the other set moves to the opposite side. Thus, as the cell divides, each reproductive daughter cell has half as many chromosomes as the parent's somatic cells. When a cross is made with two plants of the same species, like chromosomes readily pair up and meiosis proceeds normally. When the prospective parents have dissimilar sets of chromosomes, the success of the cross and the degree of sterility in any prospective progeny is dependent on the extent of the dissimilarity. The chromosomes of most interseries and many interspecies hybrids are too dissimilar to pair, like with like, and hence meiosis does not produce proper gametes.

Theoretically, sterility may be overcome by doubling the total number of chromosomes of the sterile hybrid or of the two parent plants. This is accomplished by using colchicine to create amphidiploids (allotetraploids) with four sets of chromosomes in the somatic cells and two sets instead of one in the pollen cells and egg cells. When the two tetraploid plants of different species are crossed, enough similar chromosomes exist to permit pairing, and meiosis proceeds as it should.

The early work of Dykes, Perry, and Wallace in crossing species of series *Sibiricae* and series *Californicae* was a major event in the history of siberian irises. Amos Perry's 'Margot Holmes' resulted from a cross of *Iris douglasiana* of series *Californicae* and *I. chrysographes* of series *Sibiricae*; that it was voted the British Dykes Award in 1927—the first iris to receive that honor—shows that wide-cross hybrids were highly regarded at the time. Subsequent interest in them waned, however, until an article by Lee Lenz (1959) and a chance seedling in the garden of her neighbor Leona Mahood—with features suggesting that it was a hybrid between a *Californicae* and a 40-chromosome siberian iris—incited

Jean Witt of Seattle, Washington, to undertake an extensive interseries breeding program (Witt 1959, 1971b, 1978). She was soon joined in these efforts by Lorena Reid of Springfield, Oregon, and others. Many lovely hybrids resulted from these efforts (Plate 34), but as would be expected in diploid interseries hybrids, all are sterile.

Tomas Tamberg of Berlin, Germany, began in 1972 to use colchicine to obtain tetraploid siberian irises, and later started making interseries crosses between the *Californicae* and 40-chromosome siberian irises. In 1976 he treated sterile diploid seedlings from a cross of his 40-chromosome siberian iris 'Berliner Riesen' by *Iris fernaldi* of series *Californicae* with colchicine. Three seedlings were converted to the polyploid state and proved fertile when crossed with each other (Tamberg 1990). Thus, putting theory to practice, fertile tetraploids were obtained and a new era of Calsibe hybridizing became possible. Tamberg has continued this line of breeding with fertile Calsibe seedlings, and many beautiful flowers of this type have been achieved (Plate 35). The tetraploid Calsibes are fertile with each other, producing fertile tetraploid seedlings. They also backcross successfully with tetraploid siberians of the 40-chromosome group and with tetraploid *Californicae*, but the seedlings resulting from those crosses are sterile because they have one quarter of their chromosomes from one of the parent series and three quarters from the other. Such disproportionate numbers of chromosomes cannot pair, and hence meiosis cannot proceed normally. Tamberg (1994) has very rarely obtained a viable seed from such crosses, but although the resulting seedlings have grown vigorously, they, in turn, have been sterile.

Tamberg has also succeeded in obtaining wide-cross hybrids between 28-chromosome siberian irises as pod parents and *Iris setosa* as pollen parent. Through the use of colchicine, he has converted the sterile diploids to fertile tetraploid plants, which intercross to produce excellent seedlings. He has succeeded similarly in obtaining hybrids from tetraploid crosses of 40-chromosome siberian irises and *I. lactea*, which cultivars have the very desirable characteristic of being fragrant. He continues his efforts with other wide crosses, intensively using 28-chromosome siberian irises with *I. versicolor* and 40-chromosome siberian irises with *I. setosa* and *I. prismatica*. He has also obtained hybrids between other iris species, such as *I. versicolor* and *I. laevigata*, *I. setosa* and *I. laevigata* and irises of the *Californicae* group with *I. lactea* and *I. setosa* (Tamberg 1992). As with the tetraploid Calsibes, tetraploid forms of these hybrids cross with their siblings and other similar seedlings, yielding fertile progeny, but seedlings from backcrosses are sterile.

Wide crosses often do not succeed, and even when such a cross does result in a pod, the seeds often do not germinate if planted in the usual way. Tamberg uses embryo culture to improve germination rates; the special role embryo culture plays in overcoming the relative inability of these seeds to germinate is explained in the next chapter.

Chapter 10

Seeds
and
Seedlings

Harvesting seeds

As the seed pods turn brown and near maturity, a close watch must be kept to make sure that they are harvested before they open enough to spill seeds. A fairly good rule is to pick them when the stem at the base of the pod turns from green to brown. If they must be left unattended for a week or more but seem not fully mature, a loose netting, such as a piece of an old nylon stocking or cheesecloth, can be tied around them to catch any seeds that might fall in the interim. Several months must pass after a cross is made before the seeds reach full maturity; still, it is worthwhile to attempt to save a pod that is accidentally broken off while still green and immature. Place it under lights or in a sunny window, with any remaining stem submerged in water. If no stem is attached, it is better merely to leave the pod in a warm, sunny spot, as the pod is very apt to become mildewed if it touches water directly. Even a pod broken off only a month after the cross may yet mature a few viable seeds.

The germination inhibitor

Nature has provided a protection for plants in the wild to keep their seeds from sprouting too soon after they have fallen to the ground. Except in regions with mild winter temperatures, tiny seedlings from seeds germinated in the late fall would probably not survive until spring. The protection is provided by a natural inhibitor in the seed that forestalls germination. The inhibitor is gradually inactivated, and thus the seed is prevented from sprouting that fall or winter but is ready to germinate in the spring. The existence of the inhibitor must be taken into account by the hybridizer in preparing the seeds for planting.

Planting outdoors

Most gardeners still do their planting out of doors. In northern gardens, in spite of the protection given by the inhibitor, it is best to postpone planting the seeds until October or November. This timing provides additional assurance that the seeds will not germinate too early. In southern gardens, where early germinating seedlings can survive the mild winter, the fresh, moist seeds are usually planted shortly after the pods are harvested. Some germinate that fall and more sprout in the spring.

Some gardeners plant the seeds directly in the beds, but this is unusual. Every seed cannot be expected to germinate, and therefore if seeds are planted in the row where they are to remain, empty spaces inevitably occur. The common practice is to plant the seeds in pots or flats, which enables the gardener to line out the seedlings when they are ready, usually when they are 3 to 5 inches (7.5 to 12 centimeters) tall.

Most of the various commercial growing mixes are satisfactory so long as one chooses a germinating mix, not a coarser transplanting mix. I have compared the two, planting seeds from the same crosses in both mix types, and have found that germination is much better when a germinating mix is used. An advantage of the prepared mixes is that they are relatively sterile. One can make one's own germinating mix by combining good soil, fine vermiculite, thoroughly matured compost, and fine sand in equal parts. Sift all elements together to ensure a fine texture, and sterilize the finished mix by heating in the oven at 300 degrees Fahrenheit (147 degrees Celsius) for an hour or more.

If pots are used for starting the seeds, a separate pot, adequately labeled, can be used for each cross. If flats are used for seeds of more than one cross, the seeds should be at least 1 inch (2.5 centimeters) apart in rows 2 inches (5 centimeters) apart to avoid mixing up the resulting seedlings. Even with a label identifying each set of seeds, it is best to keep a "map" of the flat in case labels are lost over winter. Plant the seeds approximately 0.5 inch (1 centimeter) deep. If a cold frame is available, place the flats in it, and as cold weather comes, apply a thick mulch to prevent the seeds from being heaved. Pots can be kept over winter in the same way or, better, they can be buried up to their rims in the garden and then mulched. In the spring, remove the mulch, move the pots to the cold frame, and put on glass or plastic covers to speed germination. As an alternative, the seeds can be stored over winter and planted in pots or flats in the spring.

Seed storage

Seeds that are to be planted outdoors in the spring or that are to be started indoors sometime over winter must be held until ready for planting. Only healthy seeds should be stored. Seeds that have been subjected to fungal or bacterial infection cannot be expected to germinate, or to survive if they do. The first step is to examine the seeds and discard any that are moldy or that have the appearance of being empty. Normal, healthy seeds are quite resistant to infections, but nonviable ones are prone to infection, which can then be spread to their neighbors. I make it a practice to dust the seeds very lightly with the fungicide thiram before placing them in plastic sandwich bags, with a few drops of sterile water, for storage. The risk of infection in the stored packets is actually quite small, provided all moldy and apparently nonviable seeds are discarded, but the fungicide lowers the risk still further. As always, observe the safety precautions prescribed by the manufacturer when using any fungicide.

In order to rid seeds of the inhibitor that prevents germination, seeds should be stored under conditions that will best lead to the inhibitor's inactivation. Unfortunately, these conditions for seeds of siberian irises are at present uncertain. It has long been known that cold storage, known technically as stratification, is needed to destroy the inhibitor in seeds of some plants—daylilies, for example. In 1973 I carried out experiments on seeds of japanese irises with clear results. When planted in germinating mix at 70 degrees Fahrenheit (21 degrees Celsius), seeds that had been stored in a slightly moist state at approximately 40 degrees Fahrenheit (4 degrees Celsius) germinated very much better than did seeds stored in the dry state at room temperature (McEwen 1973, 1974c). I assumed that the same would be true for seeds of other irises and, hence, have since stored seeds of both my siberian and japanese irises under cold, moist conditions, a few degrees above freezing, for approximately three months before planting at 70 degrees Fahrenheit (21 degrees Celsius).

These same experiments showed that the seeds must not be frozen. In an attempt to mimic the freezing conditions that occur in nature, I stored some japanese iris seeds continuously in the freezer for two months, while I kept others above and below freezing for alternate weeks. When planted, no seed from either group germinated. I have not found an adequate explanation for the lethal effect of freezing in the freezer, knowing that at least some of the seeds that fall to the ground in nature survive—protected in the ground or by debris in some way perhaps—to germinate in the spring.

Norman C. Deno is conducting extremely careful, ongoing studies of factors favoring germination. He has looked at some 2500 species of plants thus far, demonstrating strikingly different requirements among even closely related species (Deno 1994). Particularly noteworthy for growers of siberian irises are his observations on the requirements for *Iris sanguinea* and *I. sibirica*. Seeds of *I. sanguinea* germinated at only 40 degrees Fahrenheit (4 degrees Celsius) after moist storage at 70 degrees Fahrenheit (21 degrees Celsius); light had no effect. In contrast, seeds of *I. sibirica* stored in the dry state at 70 degrees Fahrenheit (21 degrees Celsius) germinated best at 70 degrees Fahrenheit (21 degrees Celsius) and required light (although fresh seeds germinated in the dark). Deno has not yet studied seedlings from crosses of those two species, which are the most common siberian irises grown.

If seeds are to be stored in the cold, therefore, the length of time needed for the cold treatment is most likely different for different seeds. In one set of trials, in which seeds of japanese irises were germinated in folds of wet paper towels in plastic pouches, 20 percent of the seeds stored in the refrigerator for three weeks germinated compared with 78 percent of those stored for nine weeks (Ahrens 1994). I generally leave the packets of moist seeds in the refrigerator from the time the seeds are removed from the pods, usually in November, until planting at 70 degrees Fahrenheit (21 degrees Celsius), approximately three months later. In view of Deno's experiments, however, I must note that from the time the pods are picked in late August or early September until the seeds are stored in the refrigerator in November, they are at room temperature and, hence, have a period of dry storage at approximately 70 degrees Fahrenheit (21 degrees Celsius) prior to the cold, moist storage.

I close this discussion of seed storage with several practical comments. Though I have been satisfied with my method of storing seeds, two extremely experienced hybridizers of siberian irises report that neither cold nor moist conditions are needed and that both siberian iris seeds planted shortly after harvest and those stored dry at room temperature subsequently germinate as well as those subjected to cold, moist storage (R. M. Hollingworth 1994; Schafer 1994). These experiences lead me to conclude that, pending additional trials, siberian iris seeds can either be planted at once after harvest or stored—moist or dry, cold or at room temperature—with equally satisfactory results.

Planting indoors

Increasingly, gardeners prefer indoor planting because it allows them to get germination off to an early start. The time-honored way of starting and growing plants "indoors" for a few months until the weather permits transplanting them to the garden is to use a greenhouse, but the same result can be had by using fluorescent lights arranged in a corner of any room or, if the operation is large, in a special room arranged for that purpose. I do not have a greenhouse and so have established a "plant room" in our garage. Hence the methods described in this chapter are those I use in our indoor plant room but are all applicable, with a few obvious modifications, to starting the seedlings in a greenhouse.

Planting indoors has at least three advantages: it can lead to early bloom, it makes care of the flats relatively easy, and it permits special types of procedures and treatments that would be impossible out of doors.

The most important advantage of planting indoors is that it allows seeds to germinate earlier than they would if planted out of doors, and thus saves a year, or even two, in obtaining first bloom (McEwen 1971b; Coble 1987). If the lighted space is large enough to accommodate the replanting of the seedlings into successively larger containers as they grow, planting can start as early as one wishes that winter or even shortly after harvesting the seeds. This should allow all healthy new seedlings to bloom the second year after the cross; by contrast, plants from seeds sown outdoors in the north bloom in the third year. Although I have a rather large lighted space in our plant room, it is fully occupied by trays meant to hold the seedlings for only about three months. If kept in those trays longer, the roots of each seedling become "pot bound," and the seedling deteriorates unless it is replanted in a larger container, for which there would be insufficient room under the lights. The seedlings therefore must be transplanted outdoors directly, and since outdoor planting in our garden cannot begin until late May, our indoor planting cannot begin until late February. Even so, the seedlings make good-sized plants in their first year and approximately 20 percent of the siberian irises and 80 percent of the japanese irises bloom the second year.

As to planting methods and care, choose a mix specially designed to promote germination. I use flats consisting of small individual compartments approximately 1.5 inches (3.5 centimeters) square at the top, planting one seed in each cell. The seedlings will be in these flats for several months and if two or more are planted together, their roots become so intertwined that they cannot be separated without considerable damage. One sort of flat, sometimes referred to as an accelerated propagation system, sits on wicklike cloth that dips into water, making it essentially self-watering. Another type, the groove tube tray, has individual compartments approximately 2 inches (5 centimeters) wide at the top and 3.5 to 5.5 inches (8.5 to 13.5 centimeters) deep that sit continuously in water or weak (one-quarter strength) fertilizer solution. I have had especially good success with the groove tube trays that are 4.5 inches (11 centimeters) deep, but if the seedlings are to remain in the flats for very much longer than three months, the deeper size would be better. Sources of these flats are listed in Appendix C. If a number of ordinary flats are used, have metal trays made, each large enough to hold several flats at once. Water poured into the metal trays waters the seedlings in the flats from the bottom.

Flats customarily last for several years; hence to avoid fungal or other infection, sterilize them after each use. Soak the flats in a solution of hypochlorite bleach, 6 ounces (180 milliliters) per gallon (3.8 liters) of water. Wash down the walls, ceilings, and floor of the plant room with a similar solution at the start of each season.

For about two weeks, the sprouted seedlings are fed by the endosperm in the seeds and no fertilizer is needed. A mix containing soil or compost will sustain the seedlings for another few weeks. If a commercial germinating mix that does not contain fertilizer is used, however, a soluble fertilizer can be started, according to the manufacturer's direction, when the tiny sprouts appear above the planting mix. Apply the fertilizer solution approximately every ten days, instead of water, for the seedlings in the ordinary type of flats. Use only a quarter- to a half-strength solution for the self-watering flats and the groove tube flats standing in the solution, for those seedlings are being fertilized continuously.

If one has only a few seedlings, it is possible to grow them in pots or flats in a sunny window, turning them daily to prevent their leaning toward the light. Still better, one can arrange metal foil at the back and sides of the tray, so that the sunlight is reflected more or less equally on all sides. For larger numbers of seedlings, artificial lighting is essential. Even if one has a greenhouse, it is helpful to have supplemental lighting, and in the absence of a greenhouse, artificial lighting is mandatory. Special fluorescent lights are made for growing plants, but one can also use a pair of ordinary fluorescent lights, one a cool white and the other a warm white (daylight) type. It is convenient to have the lights controlled by a timer that keeps them on sixteen hours daily; alternatively, they can be left on constantly. The lights do not need to be started until the seedlings begin to show above the surface of the germinating mix, but germination may be somewhat better if they are turned on as soon as the seeds have been planted (McEwen 1973). If possible, have the lights suspended by ropes from pulleys on the ceiling so they can be raised as the seedlings grow taller; keep the lights approximately 4 inches (10 centimeters) above the leaves.

A good starting temperature for the room is 70 degrees Fahrenheit (21 degrees Celsius). After germination is completed, the temperature can be reduced to approximately 65 degrees Fahrenheit (18 degrees Celsius). Having the temperature controlled by a thermostat is very helpful. As the weeks pass, the heat from the lamps and humidity from the moist germinating mix combine to increase the temperature and dampness of the room, making it necessary to lower the thermostat still further and provide ventilation.

Lining out

A few weeks before planting the seedlings in the garden rows, one should start hardening them off, that is, start to accustom them to the real world outside. Move the flats outdoors on warm days, gradually increasing the number of hours, or if a cold frame is available, move the flats to it and open its top gradually and longer on good days. If the seedlings received constant feeding while under the lights or in the greenhouse, reduce the amount of fertilizer for several weeks before the trays are moved outdoors or to the cold frame. An important purpose in the hardening process is, of course, to acclimate the pampered seedlings to colder temperatures out of doors, but that is only part of the need. The seedlings must also be gradually accustomed to sun, wind, and, usually, less consistent amounts of water and of fertilizer.

If the garden soil is a good loam, line out the seedlings when they are 3 to 4 inches (7.5 to 10 centimeters) tall; if the soil is sandy, wait until the seedlings have reached a height of 4 to 5 inches (10 to 12 centimeters). If it is not possible to plant the seedlings in the garden at that time, they should be replanted—transferred from the flats to larger containers—lest they become "pot bound."

Prior to lining out, till or dig and rake the rows that are to receive the seedlings. Water the planting mix in the flats well, so that it will come out of the flat with the seedling in one ball. A small kitchen fork can be used to lift the seedlings out with little disturbance to the roots. The flats I find most useful have holes at the bottom of each little compartment large enough to permit pushing the seedling up with a finger or stick, causing essentially no disturbance, which is still better.

Since the plants will most likely remain in place for three years or even more, they should be planted at least 9 inches (22 centimeters) apart; if space permits, 12 inches (30 centimeters) is better. If the bed is so small that it can be cared for without actually entering it, the rows need be only 24 inches (60 centimeters) apart, but in a larger bed allow a minimum of 30 inches (75 centimeters) to permit walking and working between the rows. In each small hole made for the seedlings, I like to make a nest of wet growing mix to help accustom the little plant to its new environment. The seedlings are then well settled in place with water or half-strength soluble fertilizer. A weak solution of root-stimulating hormone, such as naphthylacetic acid, at this time also helps get the seedling off to a good start. Provide partial shade by screening on sunny days for the first week or more, especially in hot regions. Take care the entire first year to ensure that the seedlings are never allowed to become dry; it is our practice to place a soaker hose along the rows of seedlings and water them well at least every other day. After the seedlings have had three or four weeks to become settled, lightly fertilize them with granular fertilizer. In addition, apply a soluble fertilizer approximately every three weeks until fall to encourage vigorous growth.

Since small seedlings are prime targets for cutworms and slugs, they may need special protection in gardens where those pests are a problem.

If the seedlings are not too numerous, they can be individually protected with 3-inch (7.5-centimeter) sections cut from the central spool of a roll of paper towels. If there are too many seedlings to make this practical, sprinkle the ground around the plants with carbaryl for the cutworms and set out slug bait for the slugs. If cutworm damage occurs—that is, the small seedlings or leaves have been cut off at the base—dig carefully around the plant with a small hand fork to find and destroy the culprit.

Embryo culture

This special type of plant propagation is particularly useful with seeds that do not germinate, or germinate poorly, in a germination mix, and hence it is especially beneficial to seeds from interseries and interspecies crosses, which often do not sprout if treated in the usual way.

In embryo culture, the embryo is removed from the seed with a dissecting needle and forceps and placed on a culture medium, in a small bottle. The whole process must be carried out under aseptic conditions to prevent contamination of the culture medium with fungi or bacteria. Air currents that could carry such contaminating agents should be avoided. A well-lighted room reasonably free of fungal spores and bacteria is usually suitable.

The culture medium consists of a solution of nutrient salts and sugar required for growth, suspended in a jellylike material of agar dissolved in hot water. While still liquid, approximately 1 inch (2.5 centimeters) of the medium is poured into small sterile bottles and allowed to cool and become firm.

The embryos are more easily removed if the seeds are soaked in water a few days. The seed is held with sterilized forceps and opened with the sterilized dissecting needle. The embryo—readily seen, close to the hilum (attachment end) of the seed—is lifted out with the needle and placed on the culture medium in one of the bottles.

The embryos are germinated in darkness at 80 to 86 degrees Fahrenheit (26 to 30 degrees Celsius) for three or four days, and then the bottles are exposed to moderate light for another week before being placed under full light, with temperature reduced to 78 degrees Fahrenheit (25 degrees Celsius). Within four to six weeks the seedlings will have developed good roots and leaves and are ready to be planted in regular growing mix in flats. Their subsequent care is as previously described for seedlings started in germinating mix.

Embryo culture varies somewhat in details of technique as carried out by different users. The specifics of preparing the culture medium and other steps of one standard method are presented in *Garden Irises* (Randolph 1959).

Tissue culture

This very special laboratory form of plant propagation is not entirely appropriate for this chapter because it involves small pieces of plants rather than seeds or seedlings; it has features in common with embryo culture, however, and can be conveniently discussed here. Tissue culture of plants has been used for many years but only recently for irises. A bulbous iris was grown this way by Baruch and Quak (1966), and the method was later applied to tall bearded irises (Meyer et al 1975). Two different parts of the plant—young inflorescences and the meristem—are used for different purposes (Vaughn 1978).

The more common type of tissue culture involves young inflorescences and has as its purpose the quick production of a large number of plants of a given cultivar without damaging the natural growth of the parent plant. The young flower stalk is cut off at its base when 5 to 6 inches (12 to 15 centimeters) tall and washed first with sodium hypochlorite and then with sterile water. All the remaining steps must be carried out with aseptic technique. The stalk is trimmed of spathes and cut into discs approximately 0.05 inch (1.5 millimeters) thick. The small discs of tissue are placed in a special growing medium in the dark (Meyer et al 1975). Growth of undifferentiated tissue known as callus develops in six to twelve weeks. The callus is then cut into several pieces, which are placed in a similar medium under light. Plantlets form at the edges of the callus; they eventually develop good roots and can be planted in ordinary growing mix when of suitable size. Many tissue discs can be cut from the single prepared stalk, resulting in a quantity of new plants.

The less common sort of tissue culture propagation is meristem culture. The meristem is the growing point at the crown of the plant; it consists of undifferentiated tissue from which the leaves and flowering stalks grow. The subject plant is disinfected with sodium hypochlorite solution and washed with sterile water. The meristem is then exposed by removing the leaves down to the inmost tiny ones. The small meristem is removed with microscalpels under magnification and is placed in a special tissue culture growing medium (Smith and Murashige 1970), where it grows to a size suitable for transplanting in ordinary growing mix.

This type of tissue culture usually results in only one plant (although four or more may be obtained with orchids), but its particular virtue is that the resulting plant can be free of viruses and other infectious agents. This is because the meristem has little or no vascular system, and hence pathogens are unlikely to invade it. Since viruses, especially, appear to be a rare problem in siberian irises, meristem culture is probably of little importance to siberian breeders. It can be used, however, to induce polyploidy. Ichie (1991), using aseptic technique, cuts a tiny square of tissue from the growing meristem culture and treats it with colchicine before returning it for continued growth in the culture medium.

Chapter 11

Judging
and
Awards

Horticultural societies have a duty to develop experienced judges who can evaluate plants of interest to their members and pass judgment on them. For irises, the responsible agency in the United States is the American Iris Society, with a roster of more than 800 members who through training and experience have qualified for various titles of judgeship. The society publishes a *Handbook for Judges and Show Officials* (American Iris Society 1985), which gives the adopted rules for judging all types of irises; the section on rules governing siberian irises was prepared by members of the Society for Siberian Irises. Readers who are interested in detailed discussions of judging are referred to this handbook; we are concerned here only with general principles of judging.

Judging is of two principal sorts: garden judging (concerned with the evaluation of plants growing in the garden, chiefly new seedlings) and show judging (concerned with the quality of individual stalks exhibited on the show bench). A separate type of show judging deals with floral arrangements, another with unnamed seedlings.

Garden Judging

Rules and standards for judging are essential as guides but should not be so rigid and restrictive as to lead to stereotyped plants and flowers.

Fortunately, the early leaders of the Society for Siberian Irises believed in diversity, and this liberal view has continued.

The plant

Obviously, it is essential that the plant as a whole be healthy and handsome, with clean green leaves in upright and gracefully arched position. One of the excellent features of siberian irises is the fine appearance of the leaves throughout the entire growing season. The leaves of an occasional plant sprawl out in late summer; such a plant deserves no place in the garden. Stalks must be tall enough to hold the flowers above the leaves; flowers that appear to float just above the leaves are particularly charming. Stalks that tower above the leaves can be useful toward the back of the garden, but most growers prefer flowers not more than 4 to 6 inches (10 to 15 centimeters) above the leaves. All these types are desirable, but stalks that carry flowers down among the leaves are a serious fault. Well-branched stalks with an occasional flower too low can, however, be accepted.

Branching

Good branches hold their flowers away from the stalk and other flowers and lift their flowers above the leaves. Indeed, any branching that is not too low is a positive attribute. On the other hand, it must be realized that the chief value of branching is to increase the number of buds—and thus lengthen the season of bloom. Hence an unbranched plant with the valuable trait of continuing or repeat bloom can be better than a branched one even though it may have only two buds at the terminal position. Stalks on continuing or repeat bloomers continue to appear over a period of four to ten weeks, which is ideal, but unfortunately, these traits are not apt to be recognized by the judge unless several visits are made to a garden. Indeed, even then it is apt to go unnoticed unless the garden host brings it to the judge's attention.

Flowers

All colors are equally desirable in judging so long as they are clear and bright. New colors and colors closer to the true spectrum hues deserve special commendation. Flowers with velvety or diamond-dusted texture, harmonious bicolor and bitoned effects, attractive signal areas, and other patterns also merit special attention.

All flower forms are acceptable so long as the total effect is pleasing and balanced. Since 'White Swirl' was introduced, flowers with similar round, flaring form have been a major attraction to judges and hybridizers, so much so that more and more 28-chromosome siberian irises introduced each year are of that type. It is a most appealing form, certainly, but it would be sad if the other graceful types should be abandoned; hybridizers should be encouraged to work toward improved flowers of all forms.

What constitutes good substance in siberian irises depends on flower form. Flowers with wide, flaring falls need strong substance. In contrast, flowers of the more traditional type, with semi-pendent or gracefully arching form, are better with lighter substance, which permits them to flutter a bit and complements their more delicate and dainty appearance.

Novelty

Novelty is another feature that deserves special consideration in garden judging, spurring hybridizers to develop new features, such as new and improved colors; new forms, such as those with six falls; better branching; longer bloom; fragrance; tetraploids; and wide-cross hybrids. Such cultivars should not be considered for awards above High Commendation, however, unless they also meet other judging standards.

Faults

I end this section on garden judging with a recapitulation of serious faults. Plants with leaves that sprawl out as the season advances deserve no consideration. Neither does a cultivar that has poor durability, one that is handsome only a day or two or is unduly damaged by sun and rain. Muddy, unattractive colors and flowers that are held down among the leaves are clearly undesirable. A less obvious but also serious fault is the fortunately rare tendency for two flowers at the terminal or a branch to open at nearly the same time and crowd each other. No matter how outstanding a cultivar may be in other ways, it should not be considered for awards if it has any of these serious faults.

Show Judging

The essential difference between garden judging and show judging is that the garden judge is critically evaluating the various cultivars whereas the show judge is primarily evaluating the skill of the exhibitors in growing and exhibiting the stalks they have brought to the show. The special rules for show judging apply only to named cultivars; floral arrangements and unnamed seedlings are evaluated differently. These various aspects of the iris show are discussed more fully in the next chapter.

Awards

Siberian irises receive awards from societies in several countries. In the United States, the awarding agency is the American Iris Society. The awards are of three types: garden awards, convention awards, and show awards. The rules governing all three types of awards to siberian irises are summarized in Table 11-1.

Garden awards

Garden awards are given on the basis of votes cast by accredited garden judges who have evaluated the growing plants in gardens. The rules governing garden awards were revised by the American Iris Society in November 1992. Those that apply to siberians irises follow.

High Commendation (HC): Only unintroduced irises may be awarded a High Commendation. Five votes are required for the award, and judges may single out as many cultivars for this distinction as they choose. An iris can receive the award as many times as it is voted until it is introduced.

Honorable Mention (HM): Siberian irises become eligible for an Honorable Mention three years after introduction and remain eligible for three more years. If the award is not received within the three-year period, the iris continues to be eligible by write-in votes. Judges vote for 10 percent of those listed, including write-ins, and the award goes to the 10 percent of the total number listed that receive the highest number of votes. If fewer than twenty are listed, the judges cast two votes each, and at a minimum, two cultivars receive the award.

Award of Merit (AM): Siberian irises become eligible for the Award of Merit two years after receiving an Honorable Mention and remain eligible for three more years. Judges vote for 10 percent of those listed, and the award goes to the 10 percent of the total number listed that receive the highest number of votes. If fewer than twenty are listed, the judges cast two votes each, and at a minimum, two cultivars receive the award.

Morgan-Wood Medal: The highest award specifically for a siberian iris is the Morgan-Wood Medal (until 1984, the Morgan Award). The medal is named for two hybridizers, Canadian F. Cleveland Morgan and Ira Wood, a very active and influential member of the American Iris Society who was especially interested in siberians. Eligibility begins two years after receiving an Award of Merit and continues for three more years. Each judge is allowed one vote, and the cultivar with the highest number of votes receives the medal. In the event of a tie, duplicate awards may be given. A list of the irises that have received the Morgan Award and the Morgan-Wood Medal concludes this chapter.

Dykes Memorial Medal: All irises that win one of the special named medals given to the cultivar judged best for each type of iris (such as the Morgan-Wood Medal for siberian irises) become eligible for the Dykes Medal the year after receiving the special medal award and remain eligible for three years. The award can be given only to an iris originating in the United States. Each judge is allowed one vote, and the iris with the highest number of votes receives the medal. In the event of a tie, a run-off ballot is issued listing the two contenders. Through 1994 the Dykes Memorial Medal has been awarded in the United States only to bearded irises, but in Britain the very first Dykes Award given by the British Iris Society went to Amos Perry's Calsibe 'Margot Holmes' in 1927, and in later years, the award was won by Marjorie Brummitt's lovely light blue siberian iris 'Cambridge' (1971) and her white 'Anniversary' (1979).

Convention awards

Convention awards are given to irises seen and voted on in the tour gardens during the annual American Iris Society conventions, with votes being cast not only by accredited judges but by all members attending the convention. The Franklin Cook Cup is given to the iris originated and introduced outside the host region that receives the highest number of votes. The President's Cup is given similarly to the iris originated and introduced within the host region. Because most attendees of the American Iris Society's conventions are enthusiasts of tall bearded irises, these awards almost invariably have gone to these plants. It was a most distinguished honor, therefore, for William McGarvey's siberian iris 'Dewful' to win the President's Cup in 1970 and for Robert Hollingworth's 'Strawberry Fair' to receive the Franklin Cook Cup in 1994.

Show awards

Show awards are given on the basis of votes cast by accredited show judges at accredited iris shows. Exhibition certificates are awarded to cultivars, unnamed seedlings, and artistic floral arrangements selected by the judges at that show. Judges may vote for an unlimited number of specimens; all those correctly entered are eligible. Five votes are required for a specimen to receive an award. See the next chapter for more details on the iris show and its special areas of competition.

Table 11-1. Rules governing awards to siberian irises.

	Eligibility	Votes required	Number judge votes for	Duration of eligibility
Garden Awards[a]				
High Commendation (HC)	any iris not yet introduced	5	any number	until introduced
Honorable Mention (HM)	3 years after introduction		10% of those listed	3 years; then eligible for write-in vote
Award of Merit (AM)	2 years after receiving HM		10% of those listed	3 years
Morgan-Wood Medal	2 years after receiving AM		1	3 years

	Eligibility	Votes required	Number judge votes for	Duration of eligibility
Dykes Medal	special medal winners of all classes, year following award		1	3 years

Convention Awards[b]

	Eligibility	Votes required	Number judge votes for	Duration of eligibility
Franklin Cook Cup	exhibited irises originated and introduced outside host region		1	during convention
President's Cup	exhibited irises originated and introduced within host region		1	during convention

Show Awards[c]

	Eligibility	Votes required	Number judge votes for	Duration of eligibility
Exhibition Certificate	all correctly entered irises at show	5	any number	during show

[a] Voted by accredited garden judges.
[b] Voted by all members attending convention.
[c] Voted by accredited show judges.

Winners of the Morgan Award and Morgan-Wood Medal, 1951–1994

The winners of the Morgan Award and the Morgan-Wood Medal are listed here together with the year of the honor and the hybridizer (in parentheses). Note that the recipients of the Morgan-Wood Medal in 1986, 1987, and 1988 were cultivars that had previously received the Morgan Award. This came about in accordance with a decision by the American Iris Society: at the 1984 spring board meeting, moves to initiate an Award of Merit category for siberian rises, to raise the Morgan Award to medal status, and to change the name of the award to the Morgan-Wood Medal were all approved. To aid in this change, it was decided that for a three-year transition period, the cultivars eligible for the Morgan-Wood Medal would be limited to the Morgan Award winners of the previous nine years.

Morgan Award

1951 'Tycoon' (Cleveland)
1952 'Eric the Red' (Whitney)
1953 'Caesar's Brother' (Morgan)
1954 'Tropic Night' (Morgan)
1955–1961 no award given
1962 'White Swirl' (Cassebeer)
1963 'Snowcrest' (Gage)
1964 'Tealwood' (Varner)
1965 'Violet Flare' (Cassebeer)
1966 'Cool Spring' (Kellogg)
1967 'Blue Brilliant' (Cassebeer)
1968 'Pirouette' (Cassebeer)
1969 'Velvet Night' (Edwards)
1970 'Dewful' (McGarvey)
1971 'Super Ego' (McGarvey)
1972 'Ego' (McGarvey)
1973 'Swank' (Hager)
1974 'Grand Junction' (McCord)
1975 'Halcyon Seas' (McCord)
1976 'Orville Fay' (McEwen)
1977 'Vi Luihn' (Dubose)
1978 'Silver Edge' (McEwen)
1979 'Augury' (McGarvey)
1980 'Ruffled Velvet' (McEwen)
1981 'Butter and Sugar' (McEwen)

1982 'Steve Varner' (Briscoe)
1983 'Ann Dasch' (Varner)
1984 'Pink Haze' (McGarvey)
1985 no award given

Morgan-Wood Medal

1986 'Butter and Sugar' (McEwen)
1987 'Steve Varner' (Briscoe)
1988 'Pink Haze' (McGarvey)
1989 'Dance Ballerina Dance' (Varner)
1990 'King of Kings' (Varner)
1991 'Mabel Coday' (Helsley)
1992 'Lady Vanessa' (Hollingworth)
1993 'Jewelled Crown' (Hollingworth)
1994 'Sultan's Ruby' (Hollingworth)

Chapter 12

Siberian Irises at Home and at Show

Siberian irises lend themselves superbly to a wide variety of uses. They are invaluable in perennial beds, shrub borders, foundation plantings, and rock gardens, as well as for landscape effects on a larger scale (Plates 36 and 37). In addition, they serve excellently as cut flowers and for exhibits and artistic arrangements at flower shows.

In the Garden

The perennial bed

Because of their graceful clumping effect and foliage that remains attractive from spring through late fall, siberian irises are excellent in a mixed planting, where their slender leaves contrast admirably with the rounder leaves of companion plants. In the rare situation where the landscape plan calls for a bed featuring plants with similar foliage, a selection of the earliest and later bulbs followed by median and tall bearded irises, siberian and japanese irises, and daylilies provides color from earliest spring to late fall, especially if reblooming irises and daylilies are included.

Siberian irises vary considerably in height, allowing the most suitable plant to be selected for each part of the garden. Tall ones—such as the older 'Emperor' and the more modern 'High Standards', 'Lavender

Light', 'Pink Snowtop', 'Springs Brook', 'White Magnificence', 'White Swirl', and the 40-chromosome 'Enbee Deeaych'—go well in the back. Many are in the 20 to 30 inch (50 to 75 centimeter) range and are therefore suitable for the mid-bed areas; smaller ones—such as 'Annick', 'Baby Sister', 'Dear Delight', 'Nana', 'Little Papoose', 'Precious Doll', and 'Sassy Kooma'—do well in the front.

The different flower forms also lend themselves to particularly advantageous placement in various parts of the perennial bed. Flowers with arching falls look well when viewed both close up or at a distance, but those of flaring form are best placed in the front half of the bed, where they may be seen from slightly above. Obviously, the selection of cultivars in a range of colors assures contrast throughout the bed but so also does the selection of different forms of flowers. Those with more traditional form—with arching or even gracefully pendent falls—provide an attractive counterpoint to the more modern large, round, ruffled, and flaring types and add beauty and interest to the entire planting.

I know of no siberian irises with colors that clash incongruously. On the other hand, a most pleasing effect can be made in the mixed perennial bed in which all the selected siberians are of a single color. The scattered clumps of irises tend to unify the entire garden bed with their handsome foliage, whether in or out of bloom.

Not only do the different flower forms add vital contrast in the perennial bed; variations in the shapes of the clumps add interest as well. Clumps with very upright leaves are nicely set off by clumps of more vase-shaped form, with leaves slanting outward somewhat, and by bowl-shaped clumps, in which leaves arch gracefully in their upper thirds.

Two broad groups of companion plants to include in the perennial bed are those that bloom at the same time as siberian irises and those that bloom before and after, providing color for an extended period. Both are key. Of course, the selection of companion plants depends above all upon the gardener's preferences, but some may be suggested, starting with those that bloom with siberian irises. Pink climbing roses are lovely behind tall purple, blue, or white siberians. Clumps of the bright yellow hybrid iris 'Roy Davidson' and of the very early yellow and golden daylilies (such as 'Esperanza', 'Lemon Prelude', 'Stella d'Oro', and the species *Hemerocallis dumortieri*) are a wonderful foil to neighboring dark blue and purple siberian irises. Whether in monochromatic accord or complementary contrast, peonies and oriental poppies of various colors combine well with siberian irises, as do various types of early summer phlox, columbine, campanulas, and coral bells. Others that bloom with siberian irises include *Alchemilla mollis, Armeria, Clematis, Dianthus, Hesperis matronalis, Lilium candidum,* lupines, *Penstemon digitalis, Primula japonica, Pyrethrum,* shasta daisies, and *Thalictrum aquilegifolium.*

The gardener can choose from the many companion plants that bloom before or after siberian irises, among them the various spring bulbs, *Primula denticulata, P. polyanthus,* forget-me-nots, true lilies, daylilies, hostas, *Phlox paniculata,* autumn blooming asters, chrysanthemums, *Iberis sempervirens, Sedum spectabile,* and ornamental grasses large and small.

Other uses in the garden

Siberian irises are ideal subjects for the shrub border, adding interest and beauty when in bloom and maintaining their strong foliage presence throughout the remainder of the season. A stately clump of white irises can be a striking accent point among the green shrubs, and similar clumps of white or other colors at the edges of a shrub border, adjacent to an uncultivated area of the property, help blend the border into the larger landscape picture. They make superb specimen clumps beside the garden gate, the mailbox, the bird bath, or a favorite bench and do well as part of foundation plantings.

In a large-scale setting, siberian irises are excellent massed against stone walls and bushes. If the property includes a natural pond or stream, siberian irises—like japanese irises, *Iris pseudacorus,* and *I. laevigata*—will be extremely happy planted along the edges, with their roots in continuously moist soil, so long as their crowns are well above the water.

Finally, with the present availability of miniatures, siberian irises have a place in the rock garden as well. Such cultivars as 'Nana', 'Baby Sister', and 'Precious Doll', with 2.5-inch (6-centimeter) flowers held on stalks less than 10 inches (25 centimeters) tall, would all fit perfectly into a small-scale setting, and new dwarf hybrids are being developed all the time.

In Arrangements

Aside from their uses in various garden settings, siberian irises make excellent cut flowers. The size and various colors of their flowers, their graceful, slender leaves, and their flexible stems make them especially popular for use in both simple and elaborate arrangements (Miller 1990). For this purpose, the stalks are best cut just as the most mature bud is about to open. With the stalks in water, each flower blooms for three or four days, and hence, if spent flowers are removed, the arrangement remains attractive for a week or so. Siberian irises have long been used in this way in the home, and they are increasingly recognized as specialty cut flowers for commerce (Wadekamper 1987).

The Iris Show

Flower show exhibitions have for many years been an important activity of iris societies. Although some siberian irises are nearly always included, the shows arranged by general iris societies have been concerned in the main with tall bearded irises and only recently have there been shows with a particular focus on siberians. Where they are exhibited together, the two types of iris complement each other beautifully, but whether the shows are for combined tall bearded and siberian irises or are primarily concerned with siberians, they are instrumental in introducing the general public to the beauty of siberian irises and have played a crucial role in furthering popular interest in these plants.

Planning the show

In addition to the overall aim of providing a magnificent floral display for the enjoyment of iris enthusiasts and the general public, an important purpose of iris shows is to make it possible for exhibitors to compete for awards. In the United States these exhibition certificates are available only at shows accredited by the American Iris Society. To receive accreditation, the show must be conducted in accordance with the rules and procedures established by the American Iris Society. These are set forth in the sections "Rules and Regulations of an Iris Show" and "Presenting an Iris Show" in the *Handbook for Judges and Show Officials* (American Iris Society 1985).

A local committee responsible for arranging and supervising the show should be appointed at least two months before its proposed date. This committee usually consists of a general chairperson and the heads of various special subcommittees, such as those that set the schedule, or handle variously the judging, staging, publicity, or properties for the show; an artistic subcommittee is appointed if a section on artistic floral arrangements is planned. As soon as the schedule for the show is prepared, a copy must be sent to the American Iris Society's exhibition committee. Once the schedule is approved, entry tags, ribbons, and other items provided by the American Iris Society can be ordered.

The subcommittees involved with publicity and judging must be selected early. Time is needed for the subcommittee on judging not only to ensure the selection of highly competent judges but also to arrange for the participation of any apprentice judges who might profit from training during the show. An important responsibility of the properties subcommittee is to ensure that an ample supply of containers is on hand at the show to hold the flowers. Green wine bottles similar in size and shape do very well; alternatively, containers can be constructed out of blocks of wood, each supporting plastic tubing of suitable length and size. Wedges should also be available, to hold each iris at a favorable angle.

Selection of flowers

Most iris shows feature named cultivars. Each cultivar exhibited is judged not in comparison with other cultivars being exhibited—and indeed, not entirely in comparison with other specimens of the same cultivar at the same show—but in comparison with a standard of perfection for that cultivar in general. It is the exhibitor's skill—in the growing, selecting, and grooming of the particular cultivar—that is being judged, not the cultivar itself.

In choosing which stalks to bring to the show, the exhibitor must have in mind how they will look when in their final position on the show bench. There, each stalk will stand upright. In the garden, even though a stalk is twisted or at an angle, each blossom on it tends to point upward; such flowers will be held awkwardly when the stalk is brought upright at exhibition. Another consideration is that the lowest branch of a branched stalk must be above the top of the container at the show.

Ideally, selected stalks are cut early on the morning of the show. Choose ones that have a bud or two just starting to open. If the time and place of the show make it necessary to cut the stalks the day before, this is perfectly feasible: simply choose stalks with buds that clearly will be open the next day. Keep the stalks overnight in a cool place, with each one in a separate narrow-topped container to hold it upright. Stalks should not be put together in a large container, with each one standing at an angle; blossoms are apt to be injured, and even overnight, the position of the flower may be slightly altered.

The question of selecting stalks that can be expected to have more than one flower open for the show can be a vexing one. According to the rules governing a show of cultivars, a stalk with only one open flower is most appropriate for a cultivar that normally has only one bud open at a time; nevertheless, even the most sophisticated judge finds it difficult not to be impressed by that extra flower.

Grooming

The term "grooming" is used to refer to all acceptable steps that can be taken before the start of a show to make the total appearance of the exhibited stalk as nearly perfect as possible. Major measures have been ongoing for months, in the excellent culture the plant has received; just before the start of the show is the time for the last-minute correction of minor faults, or grooming. Spent flowers are removed, with care to preserve the spathes; brown leaf tips are snipped off in such a way as to preserve the natural shape of the leaf; any insects that are present are brushed away. Even an entire branch can be cut off, leaving the leaf that covers its stump intact. Most of the grooming can be done before transportation to the show, but even after the stalks are in place in their containers on the entry table, small adjustments, such as wiping off fingerprints, can still be made. This is also the time to make any necessary rearrangement of unopened buds. Often a bud under the fall of an open flower will push the fall out of correct position. Merely adjusting the bud so that it is between the falls will correct the symmetry of the flower.

Transportation

The fortunate but very rare exhibitor who lives within walking distance of the exhibition hall can safely hand-carry a few beautiful stalks, but those living at a distance must take special pains. It is essential to continue to keep each individual stalk in its own narrow-topped container and to so arrange them in boxes in the car that the flowers are protected from being damaged by striking each other or a part of the vehicle. One may prepare boxes with built-in compartments to hold the individual containers (usually wine bottles or something similar), or the containers can be safely wedged apart by rolled-up newspapers or other material. If stalks had to be cut the day before the show, choice buds may open on the journey. Before starting out, some experienced exhibitors wrap the opening buds gently and lightly with tissue paper held with twine or adhesive plastic tape. The wrapping is left on throughout the trip and is not removed until the stalk is placed in its container on the entry table.

Special exhibits

Siberian irises, with their size, grace, and flexible stems, lend themselves particularly well to arrangements; it is no surprise, then, that a popular attraction at many shows is a division for artistic floral arrangements. The rules of the American Iris Society naturally require that one or more irises be included, but various other flowers suitable for the chosen theme may be used as well. Judging is usually carried out by a separate team of experienced judges and is based on the artistic quality of the arrangement as a whole and its appropriateness to the theme selected for the exhibits. At most iris shows unnamed seedlings are displayed as well. Judging them is similar to garden judging: it is an evaluation of the iris's merits rather than the exhibitor's skill.

Many shows feature educational displays regarding siberian and other irises and their general culture, as well as information regarding the national society and local groups. Often and most usefully, sheets are provided, describing the culture of the particular irises displayed, and catalogs, so that interested visitors can obtain the flowers they have admired at the show. Potted plants and packets of siberian iris seed may be sold or given away as gifts. If a local group plans a sale of irises later, this is a good time to advertise the date and location of the event.

Chapter 13

Evaluation, Registration, and Introduction

Evaluation

One of the most demanding responsibilities of hybridizers is the serious evaluation of their own seedlings, leading to the subsequent registration and introduction of any deserving those distinctions. With seedlings that one may eventually register and perhaps introduce, the standards must be at least as exacting as those of garden judging; I know of no other rules to use in evaluating one's own or another hybridizer's seedlings. The hybridizer may accept for breeding purposes seedlings with minor faults that possess features that make them promising parents toward particular goals, but such seedlings should not be registered. Indeed, if their faults are serious, it is questionable whether they should even be used as breeders, lest their bad genes outweigh the possible value of the exceptional ones.

A few guiding principles may be mentioned as signposts to observe in evaluating one's own or another hybridizer's seedlings. In the first place, the hybridizer can save a great deal of time and disappointment by starting with only the best breeding stock; otherwise, several years can be wasted raising seedlings that do not merit the time and effort of evaluation. Secondly, one's evaluation can be easier if one has hybridizing goals; an outstanding seedling is obvious and easily selected, but having goals helps in the selection of the others one should keep for breeding purposes among a large pool of seedlings. Thirdly, one must take pains to observe the seedlings of other hybridizers; it is important to be familiar with what is already available so one does not introduce seedlings indistinguishable from those already on the market. Especially as the years pass, one must avoid becoming too satisfied with one's own efforts. Visiting other hybridizers and attending meetings and conventions is essential to keep abreast of what is new. Finally, even in the north, siberian iris seedlings should be expected to bloom by the third season after the seed was planted. If a seedling does not, it lacks vigor and should be discarded unless there is some important reason for giving it one more year to prove itself.

Registration

Official registration of irises, including siberian irises, did not exist until 1920. Before then, cultivars were merely selected and given names by the breeders or others and listed for sale. Inevitably, this led to confusion since several different plants might be given the same name, and there was no record of the cultivar and its characteristics except, perhaps, in the files of the individual breeders. The establishment of an official registry by the American Iris Society in 1920 for irises of all types was a major step forward. Anyone who wishes to name an iris must clear the name with the American Iris Society's registrar, to be sure that it has not already been assigned, and complete a form giving a detailed description of that cultivar and its parentage. Thus, registration provides a controlled, official record of the cultivar and its features and helps ensure that an iris with that name is unique and true to name.

The registration office of the American Iris Society serves as the international authority for the registration of all irises except bulbous types. Registration in Australia, France, Germany, Great Britain, and New Zealand is initiated through the registrar of the appropriate national iris society, who then coordinates with the registrar of the American Iris Society to complete the registration.

Anyone who wishes to register a siberian iris can obtain information and the special forms from the registrar whose name and address are listed in the *Bulletin of the American Iris Society*. Full information is published periodically in the *Bulletin of the American Iris Society*. Check lists giving the names, hybridizers, and brief descriptions of all irises registered during the appropriate time frame are published each decade by the American Iris Society. The most recent one appeared in 1992, covering registrations and introductions from 1980 through 1989 (American Iris Society 1992). In addition, annual booklets are published to list and describe the registrations of that year (American Iris Society 1994). Separate check lists have also been published for all registered siberian irises by the Society for Siberian Irises (1991).

The number of registered siberian irises is large and growing rapidly. To keep the number within reasonable bounds, hybridizers should carefully consider whether a new seedling is sufficiently different or better than ones already registered to warrant adding it to the list. This is especially true of cultivars that will not be introduced. Otherwise, the check lists record plants that are probably not available.

Introduction

Introduction is the public offering of a registered plant for sale through advertisements, catalogs, or lists. An advertisement in the *Bulletin of the American Iris Society* automatically introduces the plant. If the offering is made through some other advertisement or list, a copy must be sent to the registrar of the American Iris Society to effect introduction. The breeder will then receive an official statement that the introduction has been recorded. An iris is not eligible for an award higher than High Commendation until it has been introduced.

Chapter 14

Siberian Irises
Around the World

Information concerning historical developments and current interest in siberian irises in the United States is given in Chapter 1 and elsewhere throughout this book. This chapter treats organizational activities in the United States and gives such information as I have been able to gather about the levels of activity and interest in other countries. In all too many instances, the international news is so meager that I hesitate to present it. I do so, however, in the hope that it may draw attention to siberian irises and may prompt readers to tell me of mistakes I have made—and to provide me with additional details.

Argentina

Monica Poole reports that siberian irises are not well known in Argentina but grow well if given extra water. She tends some modern siberian hybrids from seeds I sent her years ago but finds that in most gardens, the irises encountered are more often than not older, tall bearded cultivars. Except for her own seedlings, such siberian irises as are grown also tend to be older cultivars, such as 'Perry's Blue' and 'Caesar's Brother'. There is a garden club in Buenos Aires but no society devoted to irises, no hybridizers of siberian or other irises, and no public displays.

Australia

The Iris Society of Australia is made up of four regional societies: large groups in New South Wales and Victoria and smaller ones in South Australia and West Australia. There are none in Queensland, where the climate is too hot and dry, and none in Tasmania, where there has been very little interest in siberian irises—which is unfortunate, because the climate there would suit them. Siberian irises have not done well in Sydney, New South Wales, but grow better in the inland areas. They do quite well in the capital city of Canberra, but the population there and in other inland areas is not large, and therefore the siberian irises are seen by few gardeners and have made relatively little impact. The situation is similar in Victoria, South Australia, and West Australia.

Jo Tunney writes that her siberian irises did poorly near Perth, but at a new home some 460 miles (740 kilometers) south of Perth, the siberians have flourished and are beginning to be appreciated.

Barry Blyth, who with his wife, Lesley, owns Tempo Two, one of two large Australian nurseries with particular interest in irises, reports that siberians are the least popular irises because the heavily populated regions of Australia have a climate inhospitable for growing them. He has only fifty orders or so yearly for siberian irises from a customer base of 6500.

The other large nursery that features irises is the Rainbow Ridge Nursery, owned by Graeme Grosvenor, his wife, Helen, and Helen's brother, John Taylor, in Dural, New South Wales. In the main nursery in Dural, climatic and other conditions are not ideal for siberian irises, and therefore an additional 45 acres (18 hectares) have been obtained in the central west region, where the winters—although cold—are without snow and freezing temperatures. There, large beds of siberian and japanese irises thrive. Tall bearded irises are raised in the main nursery, near Sydney, where they do well in that warmer region as they do throughout inland Australia, even inland Queensland. Japanese irises, in which Grosvenor is especially interested, grow well in Dural also. Enthusiastic about the opportunity for change, Grosvenor actively promotes siberian and japanese irises and notes that interest in them is already growing.

New japanese and siberian irises are being imported, but the Australian gardener engaged in importing plants from overseas must clear some hurdles. All imported plants must go to a quarantine station, where they are fumigated with methyl bromide before being released, and the fees for both the import certificates and for the quarantine station are very high.

Since the death of G. B. Loveridge, no one has been actively hybridizing siberian irises. Barry Blyth registered and introduced several, including 'Coolabah', which tolerates better than most Australia's typical warm, dry conditions, but he stopped breeding siberians in 1986 and later moved his nursery from its cooler situation to Pearcedale, Victoria, where bloom is scant and does not favor crossing. John Taylor of Rainbow Ridge Nursery is a noted hybridizer of louisiana irises, and Graeme Grosvenor is launching a serious hybridizing program with siberian and japanese irises.

Australia is in the southern hemisphere, and hence its spring and summer bloom season occurs during the northern hemisphere's late fall and winter. This poses the question of the best time for breeders in Europe, Japan, and the United States to ship to Australia. Loveridge believed that the best time is September and October, when the plants, after a very brief rest, will be stimulated to start growth again by the Australian spring (Loveridge 1988).

I am indebted to Elma Tilley, Jo Tunney, Barry Blyth, Graeme Grosvenor, Rodney Barwick, and Trevor Nottle for this information.

Belgium and the Netherlands

As in most countries, interest in irises in Belgium and the Netherlands is chiefly focused on the beardeds. In the Netherlands, the great bulb firms export some siberian irises for planting and as cut flowers, along with the thousands of bulbous irises destined for the same purposes, but relatively few siberian irises are to be found in private gardens, an exception being the excellent collection of Jan de la Hayze of Seidam.

In Belgium, Koen Engelen, owner of the Kawana Nursery in Ranst, near Antwerp, specializes almost exclusively in irises and has a magnificent collection of siberians, as well as japanese and bearded irises. Alphonse Van Mulders, proprietor of the Jardinart-Van Mulders at Wijgmaal-Lewen also offers several excellent siberian irises.

According to Gilbert Verswijver, an official of the Flemish Iris Society, the society sends its members a quarterly journal largely concerned with bearded irises. He has a vast collection of irises in his garden in Hoevenen. Most are tall beardeds, but he also grows some seventy japanese irises and 370 siberians. He welcomes the many people who visit the garden each year.

Koen Engelen hybridizes only japanese and bearded irises; Alphonse Van Mulders appears to be the sole hybridizer of siberians. Aside from the large plantings in the Engelen and Van Mulders nurseries and in the gardens of Verswijver and de la Hayze, no large displays of siberian irises are open to the public.

Britain

No country in the world exhibits a keener interest in irises of all types than Britain, and the British Iris Society has been a leader in fostering awareness of irises internationally. The society is concerned with all irises, but as with most countries in the West, the bearded irises capture the most attention. Siberian irises are also popular, along with the *Californicae*; the reticulatas too are widely grown, as are water irises and some other species. The society's yearbook and its newsletters are models of their types.

An increasing interest in beardless irises was clearly demonstrated by the founding of a special section of the British Iris Society, autonomous within the society and working closely with it: the Siberian, Spuria and Japanese Group, or the S. S. and J. Group, as its members call it. The group has approximately 100 members, many from other countries, and has added a subheading to its name ("Including Pacificas and Water Irises") to emphasize the broad scope of its members' interests.

The organization owes its start to the enthusiasm of Alex Back, who was joined by a dedicated group of founding members at an inaugural meeting at the Royal Horticultural Society's New Hall in June 1976. Jennifer Hewitt was elected to chair the new society, with Doris Hansford as treasurer and Alex Back as secretary. Upon Back's tragic death in an automobile accident only two months later, Joan Trevithick was elected to take his place. She served devotedly in that capacity and as editor of the group's very successful newsletter for the next eighteen years, in spite of illness. Her death in 1994 was a sad loss to all who love beardless irises.

The major public display of siberian and other irises is at the Royal Horticultural Society's garden at Wisley. Siberians are also to be seen in Saville Garden at Windsor and at other gardens open to the public, as well as in nurseries and private gardens. In addition, the National Collection of *Iris sibirica* Cultivars is held for the National Council for the

Conservation of Plants and Gardens (NCCPG) by the Shropshire Group of NCCPG as a "dispersed" collection. Members of the county group grow one or more cultivars in their own gardens, some of which are occasionally open to the public. Stock plants of all cultivars are grown by the county organizer, Kim W. Davis, at his nursery near Bucknell, where an Open Day is held in June, during the flowering season. The main categories of siberians included in the collection are British-raised cultivars, award-winning irises, and historic irises.

Awards for irises in Britain include the Dykes Medal, which is given annually to the iris judged best, as it is in the United States. In Britain, irises from all countries are eligible, except those from the United States, Australia, and New Zealand, which have their own Dykes awards. The British Dykes Medal has twice been awarded to siberian irises. The Royal Horticultural Society also has a separate system of awards, including the Award of Garden Merit, which has been won by several siberian irises.

Jennifer Hewitt is the only serious hybridizer of siberian irises in Britain. Her introductions include several 28-chromosome cultivars, and she is also known for her 40-chromosome introductions. The S. S. and J. Group and the iris world at large lost a highly skilled and dedicated member with the death in 1993 of Harry Foster, whose hybridizing efforts had led to the registration of some twenty-two siberian irises.

Interest in siberian irises continues to grow, with many nurseries offering more of the newer cultivars each year. Increasing numbers of siberians in private gardens are made possible by the seed and plant distribution programs of both the British Iris Society and the S. S. and J. Group. Information regarding membership in the British Iris Society and the S. S. and J. Group can be obtained from the secretary of the British Iris Society.

Canada

As would be expected, iris enthusiasts in Canada and the United States have many interests in common, and although Canada has its own very active and successful Canadian Iris Society, many Canadians are members of the American Iris Society and the Society for Siberian Irises. The influence of Canadians on siberian iris growers in the United States is perhaps best illustrated by the fact that the highest specific award a siberian iris can be given by judges of the American Iris Society is co-named in honor of Canadian F. Cleveland Morgan. In addition, the influence of Isabella Preston still guides breeders of siberian irises in the United States; it was her pioneering work at the Dominion Experiment Station in Ottawa in the 1930s that demonstrated the importance of making planned crosses.

Verna Laurin, secretary of the Canadian Iris Society, judges that siberian irises are second in popularity after the tall beardeds and reports that they are widely grown by the average family gardener. Each year at the auction held as part of the society's annual meeting, siberian irises are offered in ever-increasing numbers. In addition to the annual meeting, seminars and other meetings and garden visits organized by the national society and by regional and local groups are held throughout the year.

The Experimental Farm in Ottawa has a good collection of siberian irises including, of course, Isabella Preston's introductions. The Royal Botanical Garden in Hamilton has an outstanding display of some 150 different cultivars. Most members of the society include a few siberians in their gardens and some, such as Catherine Boyko of Dunnville, Verna Laurin of Willowdale, and Irene Specogna of Bolton, all in Ontario, grow many. Modern as well as older siberian iris cultivars can be obtained from McMillen's Iris Garden in Norwich, Ontario, and Les Jardins Osiris in St. Thomas de Joliette, Quebec.

Quebec boasts several very active horticultural societies but no group concerned especially with irises. Jacques Doré, an owner of Les Jardins Osiris, explains that only a few people from the French part of Canada attend functions of the Canadian Iris Society because of the distance and language barrier. His nursery, which specializes in irises and daylilies, has a large collection of siberian irises, which he updates regularly.

As for serious hybridzing of siberian irises, there is little activity at present. Alan McMurtrie of Willowdale, Ontario, is engaged in a very important breeding program with reticulatas and is interested in siberians but does not hybridize them. Hugh Pearson, former hybridizer at the Royal Botanical Garden, registered two new siberians in 1991, 'Red Royal' and 'Sapphire Royal'. Jacques Doré began hybridizing japanese and siberian irises in 1993.

Verna Laurin and Jacques Doré have kindly provided me with information for this account.

Chile

No society in Chile is concerned with irises, nor are irises widely grown there. Of those that are grown, the bearded types predominate. F. M. Schlegel, a member of the faculty of the Universidad Austral in Valdivia, created a 77-acre (31-hectare) arboretum, with several swampy sites featuring siberian and japanese irises. The climate of Valdivia, in south-central Chile, can be compared to that of southern Oregon. Rainfall is roughly 75 inches (188 centimeters) yearly, concentrated between May and September (fall and winter in Chile); siberians require extra watering during the spring and summer, when only about 2 inches (5 centimeters) of rain falls. Schlegel began with only a few older siberian irises but raised more modern cultivars from seeds sent from the United States and started a hybridizing program with them, working with Calsibes as well, using *Iris douglasiana* and *I. innominata*.

China

China and its neighbors are the native home of all 40-chromosome siberian iris species and of two of the three species that make up the 28-chromosome group, yet strange to say, public gardens in China include surprisingly few siberians in their iris displays. Among the gardens that do are Northeast Normal University (Changchun, Jilin Province), Beijing Botanic Garden, Nanjing Botanic Garden (Jiangsu Institute of Botany), Shanghai Botanic Garden, Hanzhou Botanic Garden, and Sichuan Agricultural University (Triticae Research Institute, Dujiangyan, Sichuan Province).

Zhao Yu-tang is professor of botany at Northeast Normal University and the leading authority on irises in China. He has made many contributions in his own country and, with James W. Waddick, has written *Iris of China* (1992), which is spreading knowledge of those flowers in the Western world.

Continuing scientific studies of the species of siberian irises in China are urgently needed. A plan to develop a National Collection of Chinese Irises at Nanjing Botanic Garden is underway, which effort to create an authentic collection of living plants in China itself is a most important and welcome first step toward answering many unsettled questions.

Denmark and Sweden

One Danish plant society concerns itself with irises and lilies (Dansk Iris og Liljeklub), but the president, Lars Hopfner of Roskilde, estimates that only three or four members have any special interest in siberian irises. His current project is a geographic garden in Kolding, Jutland, where a large collection of irises is being established. The intention is to display irises of a given country or region in a section of the garden representing that part of the world, and the plan is to include various siberian irises in the area devoted to Siberia, although only *Iris sanguinea* is actually native to it.

Sweden has no society especially for irises. Christian Lindner of Lidingo and Inga Brolin of Hoerby, my two informants, tell me that few people there are interested in siberians. They are aware of no public gardens growing siberian irises (except for botanical gardens, which include only a few examples of the species) and know of only one nursery that sells them (and only older cultivars are offered at that). Both grow some of the modern siberians in their own gardens. Lindner started with a few in 1990 and adds to his collection each year, including some of the newest and best.

France

The Société Française des Iris and its members are concerned with irises in general, but they are primarily interested in the bearded types. Jean Peyard of Seyssinet, a serious amateur grower of all sorts of irises, reports that siberians are not often encountered in France.

The Cayeux Nursery, however, has 2.5 acres (1 hectare) devoted to them, and such a large area indicates that they must be in some demand. The famous firm of Cayeux is in its fourth generation specializing in irises. Although their chief interest is the bearded cultivars, they grow some 30,000 siberian irises, many cultivars of which they list in a separate catalog devoted to beardless types. Jean Cayeux continued the noted nursery of his grandfather and father near Paris and in 1960 created the large nursery in Poilly-lez-Gien, which is devoted almost exclusively to irises and some daylilies; upon his retirement, his son Richard took charge of the nursery. The Bourdillon Nursery in Soings-en-Sologne is another important source of siberian irises in France.

Richard Cayeux is starting to hybridize siberian irises. The climate and growing conditions are favorable for them throughout France, except for the southern areas along the Mediterranean, where it is too warm at sea level, although suitable microclimates may be found at higher coastal elevations.

Jean Peyard and Richard Cayeux have kindly provided information for this summary.

Germany

The former Deutsche Iris- und Liliengesellschaft changed its name some years ago in keeping with its broad interest in all perennials and is now the Gesellschaft der Staudenfreunde (Friends of Perennials Society). The society is made up of eight groups, one of which is devoted to irises. The iris group has approximately 100 members and hosts an annual show at a different location each year. More and more, beardless irises—and especially siberians—have predominated at the shows, reflecting the steadily increasing interest in them.

No official display gardens of siberian irises are in place, but many fine collections can be found in the gardens of members and in public parks, such as the Palmengarten in Frankfurt. Large stands of the species *Iris sibirica* grow wild, especially in the south (McEwen 1974a).

Several important hybridizers of siberian irises are active in Germany. Eckard Berlin of Mittelbiberach began his breeding efforts in 1965, working especially with wide-cross hybrids and with colchicine to develop tetraploids. He was one of the first to bring *Iris typhifolia* to Germany. Tomas Tamberg, whose important accomplishments in the field are discussed in Chapter 9, and Artur Winkelmann, of Aindling in southern Bavaria, are particularly noted for their work with interseries hybrids. Winkelmann started with a chance cultivar among some plants of 'Niklassee', Eckard Berlin's tetraploid siberian iris. This hybrid of 'Niklassee' and *Iris versicolor*, which he has named 'Neidenstein', has crossed successfully with tetraploid siberian irises but not with diploids.

Marlene Ahlburg of Rötgesbuttel was an important hybridizer of siberian irises in the 1970s and '80s and is especially known for the yellow amoena diploids she registered in 1990. Subsequent limitations in space, however, forced her to discontinue her efforts with irises in favor of hellebores and hepaticas, which demand less room. These veteran hybridizers have been joined recently by a handful of newcomers: Harald

Moos of Hanover, Matthias Thomsen-Stork of Waldshut-Tiengen, and Helmut von Kotzebue of Hollen.

Siberian irises are available in many nurseries. Three large nurseries with a focus on irises of various types—especially siberians—are the Friesland Staudengarten of Uwe Knöpnadel in Jever, Friesland, that of Eberhard Schuster in Augustenhof, and Schöppinger Irisgartin in Schöppingen. Tomas Tamberg's outstanding garden in Berlin is a show-case for siberian irises in general and his wide-cross hybrids in particular.

Italy

The Società Italiana dell'Iris is a very active organization whose members include an extremely dedicated group charged with managing the society's famous garden in Florence. Each year the society holds the Concorso Internazionale dell'Iris, at which competition bearded irises sent three years previously from countries worldwide and grown on in the society's garden are judged for awards. Some older siberian irises grace the society's garden in Florence, but the plants found there are chiefly bearded irises, in keeping with the purposes of the annual competition.

One member of the society reports that the species *Iris sibirica* is native to Italy's northern regions and to Puglia in the south but that these wild plants are becoming rare. Siberian irises grow fairly well there, especially in the north, but are much less popular than the tall bearded irises.

No significant public or private displays of siberian irises are known. Grower Guido degli Innocenti of Florence lists siberians in his catalog, and they are also offered by various nurseries in the north. Augusto Bianco, an iris hybridizer in Turin, now includes siberian irises in his breeding program.

Japan

Seven different species of irises grow wild in Japan, namely *Iris ensata*, *I. gracilipes*, *I. japonica*, *I. laevigata*, *I. rossii*, *I. sanguinea*, and *I. setosa* (Horinaka 1992). Japanese botanists believe that all are native to Japan, with the exception of *I. japonica*, which they say was brought from China. Only three are being hybridized: *I. ensata*, *I. laevigata*, and *I. sanguinea*. *Iris ensata*, known in Japan as *hanashōbu* and in the West as the japanese iris, is the overwhelming favorite, lovingly admired by millions of Japanese people each year in what are, in essence, horticultural pilgrimages. *Iris laevigata* was originally the most popular and was the first to be illustrated, in a drawing in the 8th century. *Iris sanguinea*, known in Japan as *ayame*, grows throughout Japan and is valued as a garden plant but is the serious interest of only one hybridizer, Ho Shidara (Shimizu 1992).

Horinaka (1992) lists several forms of *ayame* in various sizes and colors; most have the characteristic features so familiar to us in the West: no branches, and leaves and flower stalks of approximately equal height. One, 'Edazaki-ayame', is branched, however, and has wider leaves than the others. Another, 'Kamayama', has deep violet flowers and stalks distinctly taller than the leaves. Horinaka (1994) believes that 'Kamayama' is a hybrid of Korean origin between *Iris sanguinea* and *I. sibirica*. The branched 'Edazaki-ayame' may well be a hybrid also. On our visit to Japan in June 1991, Hiroshi Shimizu drove us to uncultivated fields in the foothills of Mount Fuji, where we saw many clumps of native *I. sanguinea* in bloom. These were violet-blue in color, unbranched, and with leaves and stalks of similar height (Plate 10).

The most important hybridizer of siberian irises in Japan is Ho Shidara. His interest began in 1954 when he started crossing different types of the native species. Over the years Shuichi Hirao gave him some modern American and British introductions to use with his own seedlings. Some excellent plants in a variety of colors resulted, including some with six falls, which resemble double japanese irises. He also developed multipetalled cultivars with nine or more petals, which he calls *yaezaki-ayame* (Shidara 1992). Examples of these interesting flowers are shown in Plates 15 and 16. Hiroshi Shimizu, a leading hybridizer of japanese irises, also grows siberians but is prevented from hybridizing them by limited space. He too has named several multipetalled seedlings, including one discovered in a farmer's garden by the late Koji Tomino, famed breeder of Ise japanese irises; this violet flower Shimizu named in memory of Tomino. Although an occasional six-falled siberian iris appears in a seedling bed in the United States, they have not been developed further and these new types of siberian iris flowers are a distinctly Japanese contribution.

Japan has two national iris societies. The older one came about as the result of a visit George M. Reed made to Japan in 1930. Reed, curator of plant pathology at the Brooklyn Botanic Garden in New York, was active in the affairs of the American Iris Society; his suggestion that a similar society be started in Japan was enthusiastically received, and the Nihon Hanashōbu Kyokai (Japanese Hanashōbu Society) was founded. Although members of the society grow some other irises also, the main interest is the *hanashōbu*, the japanese iris. Because of this, in 1967, Akira Horinaka established a second society, the Nihon Iris Kyokai, to encourage interest in other irises. Although the names in Japanese are different, both are translated into English as Japanese Iris Society, which, of course, can lead to confusion.

Although the native types of *ayame* are grown in many gardens, there has been little interest in modern siberian iris hybrids. Several nurseries are beginning to offer some from American and English breeders, however, as well as Shidara's introductions.

I am indebted to Akira Horinaka, Ho Shidara, and Hiroshi Shimizu for their help in preparing this account.

New Zealand

The New Zealand Iris Society is an active organization with many enthusiastic members. It is divided into two sections, one concerned with bearded iris cultivars and the other with iris species, including siberian irises. Loyal member of the American Iris Society Ira Wood and his wife, Betty, made several trips to Australia and New Zealand to visit iris gardens. Upon her husband's death, Betty Wood established funds in his memory in both Australia and New Zealand to encourage continued interest in siberian irises. Her generosity has enabled the New Zealand Iris Society to donate plants to various institutions, such as secondary schools, especially those with horticulture departments. Public parks are also supplied with siberian irises, on assurance that the plantings be well cared for, permanent, and open to the public. This program has been carried out with great success.

Paul Richardson reports that siberian irises are second in popularity after the bearded types, and Frances Love, former president of the New Zealand Iris Society and an enthusiastic grower of siberians, believes that they have perhaps surpassed bearded irises. An important reason for the popularity of the siberians is the ease with which they can be grown all over New Zealand, whereas bearded irises do not bloom well in the far north and louisiana irises do poorly in the far south. The species and hybrids of subseries *Chrysographes* especially are objects of considerable interest.

Climatic conditions vary greatly in New Zealand, from north to south and east to west. The northern part of the North Island is semi-tropical, and the southern part of the South Island is quite cold in winter. A long chain of mountains extending from the middle of the North Island to the end of the South Island also influences the weather, with ample rain to the west of the mountains and drier conditions to the east. New Zealand's length contributes to its variable season of bloom, as it does in the United States, but because New Zealand is located in the southern hemisphere, the progression is the reverse of what the northern hemisphere experiences: the season of bloom begins in the north, in October and November, and concludes in the south, in February. Plants shipped from countries in the northern hemisphere do best if sent in September, when spring growth is just starting.

The late Jean Collins was particularly fond of siberian irises and selected two seedlings later named by her husband, Hector, as 'Jean's Delight' and 'Violet Blaze'. Frances Love, who is the only active hybridizer, has named three 28-chromosome siberian irises (a tetraploid and two diploids, one a standard and one miniature), and 'Blue Guest', a 40-chromosome siberian. She concentrates on siberian irises in her breeding program.

Besides the displays of siberian irises in private gardens, such as those of Frances Love in Carterton, Hector E. Collins in Taurange, and the Richardsons in Upper Hutt, there is a public display garden, Mona Vale, in Christchurch. The garden was started in 1972 through a gift made to the Christchurch city council by C. S. Thomas, an early member of the New Zealand Iris Society, "to establish and maintain a Botanic Iris Garden and . . . for the purchase of species and the latest hybrids of the genus *Iris* for planting in said garden."

Well-known nurseries that specialize in siberian irises include Bay Bloom in Tauranga, Ranch North Iris Gardens in Whangarei, and Mossburn Iris Gardens in Mossburn, Southland.

I am grateful to Frances Love and Paul Richardson for this information.

Russia

Russia can take pride in being the home country of George I. Rodionenko, former director of the botanical garden in St. Petersburg and a leader in the scientific study of irises. His scholarly books and articles on irises of all types and especially those native to the republics of the former Soviet Union have added much to our knowledge of these flowers. He is particularly interested in siberian irises and has written a book as well as many scientific articles about them.

In 1992 the Central Iris Society was founded with Sergey Loktev as the first president. By the end of 1993 there were seventy-three members. The chief interest of the society is bearded irises, with siberian irises second in popularity. Plans are being made to organize an iris competition in Moscow for tall bearded and border bearded irises.

Loktev has started crossing tall bearded irises but knows of no one engaged in hybridizing siberians. Siberian irises of subseries *Sibiricae* grow well throughout Russia. Displays of siberians and other irises can be seen in botanical gardens, especially the one in St. Petersburg, where Rodionenko collected many species and modern cultivars.

South Africa

The Iris Society of South Africa holds an annual All South Africa Iris Show each October, when the flowers are in bloom. Irises of all types are exhibited, including some siberians. The society's secretary, Matilda Anderson, reports that there has not been much interest in siberian irises but that since 1989 there has been a marked increase in the number grown, including some of the newer cultivars. Until then, only the older siberian irises, such as 'Caesar's Brother', were encountered. An obvious reason for limited interest is the climate, which is too warm for siberian irises except at the higher elevations.

No public displays are known and no one is hybridizing siberian irises, but several nurseries have some of the older cultivars and if interest continues to increase, newer ones will no doubt become available.

Switzerland

The Schweizer Iris- und Lilienfreunde has several members who grow siberians, but the group is primarily interested in the bearded irises. Climate and soil are suitable for hybrids of the 28-chromosome group. Thomas Bürge of Wabern has a collection of these plants and is an active hybridizer who has named several excellent seedlings.

United States

The founding of the Society for Siberian Irises was inspired by the late Peg Edwards's 1959 article on the status of siberian irises, which appeared in the *Bulletin of the American Iris Society* (Edwards 1959). The response from readers was so impressive that the idea of forming a special society concerned exclusively with siberian irises was born, and the Society for Siberian Irises was established in 1960 as a section of the American Iris Society. Peg Edwards was the prime mover in this enterprise and became the first president; Sarah Tiffney served as vice president, Charlotte Withers as secretary, and William G. McGarvey as treasurer. Irwin Conroe, Peggy Burke Grey, Ben R. Hager, Mildred Johnson, Virginia Melnick, Sherman Preece, Jr., Dorothy Spofford, Irene Van de Water, Eleanor Westmeyer, and Bee Warburton—who was of particular help to Peg Edwards—were members of the original board of directors and headed the various committees. Peg Edwards also served as editor of the society's journal from 1960 to 1984.

The society exists, as stated in the bylaws, to "foster the culture, appreciation, breeding, improvement and distribution of Siberian irises and hybrids involving them and to promote a spirit of cooperation and good fellowship among its members and between its members and those of other societies." Its purposes as initially envisioned have been well served.

Very soon regional groups began to form, which resulted in meetings and shows devoted to siberian irises. Over the years, the meetings of the American Iris Society, founded in 1920, gradually assumed the proportions of an annual national iris convention, with discussion groups, shows, and garden tours to view the irises that had been sent as guest plants. The dates of the American Iris Society's annual conventions are timed to show tall bearded irises at their best, and because the date of bloom for siberian irises is so close to that of the later bearded irises, some siberians were invariably included in the convention gardens. For many years there was little thought of having a separate siberian iris convention; nevertheless, the desirability of holding such a convention—where siberian irises could be seen in large numbers and at their best—became increasingly appreciated and resulted in the first Siberian Iris Convention, held in East Lansing, Michigan, in 1993, under the leadership of Robert and Judith Hollingworth and the sponsorship of the Iris

Connoisseurs of Michigan. Some 200 people attended, including two from Japan and one each from England and Germany. It was a tremendous success. The second convention is scheduled to be held in Massachusetts in 1996.

The Society for Siberian Irises publishes its journal, *The Siberian Iris*, and check lists of registered siberian irises. Information regarding membership in the Society for Siberian Irises can be obtained from the membership secretary of the American Iris Society.

Appendix A

Favorite Siberian Irises

The Society for Siberian Irises conducts a popularity poll every year or two to learn which cultivars the members consider the best. In 1992, eighty-three members—representing Britain, Canada, and twenty-seven states of the United States—voted for their fifteen favorites with the following results:

Rank	Cultivar	Number of votes
1	'Lady Vanessa'	37
2	'Jewelled Crown'	36
3	'Butter and Sugar'	33
	'Pink Haze'	33
	'Shirley Pope'	33
4	'King of Kings'	24
	'Ruffled Velvet'	24
5	'Temper Tantrum'	22
6	'Sultan's Ruby'	21
7	'Mabel Coday'	19
	'White Swirl'	19
8	'Esther CDM'	18
	'Reprise'	18
	'Springs Brook'	18
9	'Aqua Whispers'	17
	'Shaker's Prayer'	17

Rank	*Cultivar*	*Number of votes*
10	'Dance Ballerina Dance'	16
	'High Standards'	16
	'Regency Buck'	16
11	'Indy'	15
	'Jamaica Velvet'	15
	'Liberty Hills'	15
	'Super Ego'	15
12	'Percheron'	13
	'Snow Prince'	13
13	'Heliotrope Bouquet'	11
	'Tiffany Lass'	11
	'Windwood Spring'	11
14	'Pas de Deux'	10
	'Swank'	10
15	'Anniversary'	9
	'Augury'	9
	'Caesar's Brother'	9
	'Cathy Childerson'	9
	'Harpswell Happiness'	9
	'Jaybird'	9
	'Summer Sky'	9
	'Tealwood'	9

A popularity poll was held at the Siberian Iris Convention in East Lansing, Michigan, in 1993, as well. The irises voted on were those featured as guest plants in the convention tour gardens and therefore the list excludes many excellent cultivars that were not represented in those gardens. A total of 112 votes were cast by those attending the convention. The cultivars voted for (in descending order of the number of votes received) were as follows:

'Over in Gloryland'
'Jewelled Crown'
'Lee's Blue'
'Coronation Anthem'
'Moon Silk'
'Little Papoose'

'Sprinkles'
'Welfenschatz'
'Cheery Lyn'
'Roaring Jelly'
'Simple Gifts'
'Shall We Dance'
'Mabel Coday'
'Frosted Cranberry'
'Reprise'
'Springs Brook'
'Wings of Night'
'Aqua Whispers'
'Bridal Jig'
'Lady Vanessa'
'Harpswell Velvet'
'Illini Dame'
'Sailor's Fancy'
'Rill'
'Blue Reverie'
'Hubbard'
'Laughing Brook'
'Purple Sand'
'That's My Baby'
'Magenta Moment'
'Mystic Lagoon'
'Temper Tantrum'
'Lorena Cronin'
'Sassy Kooma'
'Shaker's Prayer'

One more useful list for gardeners seeking outstanding siberian irises is that of the winners of the Morgan Award and Morgan-Wood Medal, the siberian irises selected as the best each year since 1951 by judges of the American Iris Society. Many of them are rather old, but they show what was considered most outstanding in their day and all are still very good. A list of those award winners concludes Chapter 11.

Where to See Siberian Irises

The Society for Siberian Irises named a number of siberian iris display gardens in 1983. That list is being revised. The gardens shown below include those from the 1983 group whose owners wish to be included, and, in addition, new ones with excellent collections of siberian irises. I am sure others should be added to the list and regret having missed them.

In addition to the name and address, the telephone number is sometimes listed so that a prospective visitor can call in advance to select a convenient time. Those gardens to be visited only by appointment are marked with an asterisk (*) at the conclusion of their entry; if a telephone number is not given, please write for an appointment. The approximate dates of bloom are shown in parentheses. The gardens in the United States are grouped, roughly, by geographic region.

United States

• *New England*

Philip Boucher
Tranquil Lake Nursery, Inc.
45 River Street
Rehoboth, Massachusetts 02769
telephone 508.252.4002
(1 June to late June)

Elaine and Chandler Fulton
21 Hillcrest Road
Weston, Massachusetts
  02193-2020
telephone 617.891.4015
(1 June to 15 June)*

Steven D. Jones
Fieldstone Gardens, Inc.
620 Quaker Lane
Vassalboro, Maine 04985-9713
telephone 207.923.3836
(mid-June to 1 July)

Elisabeth and Currier McEwen
Seaways Gardens
RR1, Box 818
South Harpswell, Maine 04079
telephone 207.833.5438
(7 June to 1 July)*

Shirley L. Pope
Pope's Perennials
39 Highland Avenue
Gorham, Maine 04038-1701
telephone 207.839.3054
(10 June to 25 June)*

Janet Sacks and Martin Schafer
Joe Pye Weed's Garden
337 Acton Street
Carlisle, Massachusetts 01741
telephone 508.371.0173
(1 June to 20 June)

Barbara and David Schmieder
566 Old Road to NAC
Concord, Massachusetts 01742
telephone 508.369.3383
(1 June to late June)

Darlyn C. Springer
York Hill Farm
18 Warren Street
Georgetown, Massachusetts 01833
telephone 508.352.6560
(1 June to 4 July)

Cindy and Ron Valente
Valente Gardens
RFD 2, Box 234
East Lebanon, Maine 04027
telephone 207.457.2076
(mid-June to 1 July)*

Agnes and Kenneth Waite
6 Tow Path Lane
Westfield, Massachusetts
  01085-4532
telephone 413.568.7081
(late May to early July)

John W. White
193 Jackson Hill Road
Minot, Maine 04258
telephone 207.345.9532
(10 June to 25 June)

White Flower Farm
Route 63
Litchfield, Connecticut 06759
telephone 203.496.9600
(late May to late June)

Sharon Hayes Whitney
Eartheart Gardens
RR 1, Box 847
South Harpswell, Maine 04079
telephone 207.833.6327
(7 June to 1 July)*

• *Middle Atlantic*

Lynn R. Batdorf
U.S. National Arboretum
3501 New York Avenue NE
Washington, D.C. 20002
telephone 202.245.5965
(mid-May to early June)

Dana Borglum
Borglum Irises
2202 Austin Road
Geneva, New York 14456
telephone 716.526.6729
(early June to late June)

George C. Bush
Bush Gardens
1739 Memory Lane Extd
York, Pennsylvania 17402
telephone 717.755.0557
(mid-May to early June)

Kathleen and Leonard Guest
494 North Street
East Aurora, New York 14052
(10 June to 20 June)

James P. Holmes
2 Deer Hill Road
Chester, New Jersey 07930
telephone 908.879.9009
(1 June to 10 June)

Sterling Innerst
2700-A Oakland Road
Dover, Pennsylvania 17315
telephone 717.764.0281
(20 May to 20 June)

Carol Warner
Draycott Gardens
16815 Falls Road
Upperco, Maryland 21155
telephone 410.374.4788
(15 May to 5 June)*

• *South*

Everette Lineberger
Quail Hill Gardens
2460 Compton Bridge Road
Inman, South Carolina
    29349-8489
telephone 803.472.3339
(1 May to 15 May)

Suky and Clarence Mahan
The Iris Pond
7311 Churchill Road
McLean, Virginia 22101
(15 May to 1 June)*

Diana and Mike Nicholls
Nicholls Gardens
4724 Angus Drive
Gainesville, Virginia 22065
telephone 703.754.9623
(mid-May to late June)

Rosa Van Valkenburgh
212 Longwood Drive SE
Huntsville, Alabama 35801
(5 May to 21 May)*

Joe S. Watson
116 Watson Reynolds Road NE
Milledgeville, Georgia 31061
telephone 912.452.8916
(24 April to 15 May)

Ruth S. Wilder
802 Camellia Drive
Anderson, South Carolina 29625
(5 May to 20 May)

John W. Wood
2654 Prospect Church Road
Mooresboro, North Carolina 28114
telephone 704.657.5149
(15 April to 15 May)

• *Midwest*

Penny Aquirre
Coopers Garden
2345 Decatur Avenue North
Golden Valley, Minnesota 55427
telephone 612.591.0495
(10 June to 25 June)

Robert Bauer and John Coble
Ensata Gardens
9823 East Michigan Avenue
Galesburg, Michigan 49053
telephone 616.665.7500
(1 June to 15 June)*

Louise Bellagamba
11431 Old Saint Charles Road
Bridgeton, Missouri 63044-3075
telephone 314.739.5413
(15 May to 25 May)*

Ainie Busse
Busse Gardens Co., Inc.
5873 Oliver Avenue SW
Cokato, Minnesota 55321
telephone 612.286.2654
(1 June to 30 June)*

Joan N. Cooper
212 West County Road C
Roseville, Minnesota 55113
telephone 612.484.7878
(10 June to 25 June)*

Lorena and Arthur Cronin
10, 920 Oakwood Road
Roscommon, Michigan
    48653-0024
telephone 517.275.5426
(24 May to 10 July)*

James L. Ennenga
1621 North 85th Street
Omaha, Nebraska 68114
telephone 402.391.6337
(late May to late June)

Lois Girton
The Iowa Arboretum
2025 Ashmore Drive
Ames, Iowa 50014-7804
telephone 515.795.3216
(25 May to 10 June)

Anne and Dale Hamblin
152 North Idlewild
Mundelein, Illinois 60060
telephone 708.949.6822
(15 May to 27 June)*

Larry L. Harder
208 First Street
Ponca, Nebraska 68770
telephone 402.755.2615
(20 May to 15 June)*

David Heschke
Heschke Gardens
11503 77th Street South
Hastings, Minnesota 55033
telephone 612.459.8381
(late May to late June)*

Judith and Robert Hollingworth
Windwood Gardens
124 Sherwood Road East
Williamston, Michigan 48895
telephone 517.349.8121
(1 June to 15 June)

Kit and Roy Klehm
Klehm Nursery of Champaign
4210 North Duncan Road
Champaign, Illinois 61821
telephone 800.553.3715
(15 May to 1 June)

Anna Mae and Ronald Miller
Old Douglas Perennials
6065 North 16th Street
Kalamazoo, Michigan 49007
telephone 616.349.5934
(26 May to 20 June)*

Kevin J. Morley
Phoenix Gardens
8404 Cherry
Kansas City, Missouri 64131
telephone 816.523.4849
(15 April to 15 June)*

Donald R. Sorensen
5000 Eleven Mile Road
Rockford, Michigan 49341
telephone 616.866.1493
(mid-May to mid-June)*

Harold L. Stahly
8343 Manchester Drive
Grand Blanc, Michigan 48439
telephone 810.694.7139
(5 May to 15 May)

Lynn and Barrett Stoll
Walnut Hill Gardens
999 310th Street
Atalissa, Iowa 52720
telephone 319.946.3471
(20 May to 10 June)*

Florence Stout
150 North Main Street
Lombard, Illinois 60148
telephone 708.627.1421
(1 June to 20 June)*

Steve Varner
Illini Iris
Route 3, Box 5
Monticello, Illinois 61856
telephone 217.762.3446
(7 May to 10 June)*

Julius Wadekamper
Borbeleta Gardens
15980 Canby Avenue
Faribault, Minnesota 55021
telephone 507.334.2807
(1 June to 30 June)

Melody and Jerry Wilhoit
Redbud Lane Iris Garden
Route 1, Box 141
Kansas, Illinois 61933
telephone 217.948.5478
(15 May to 15 June)

• *Rocky Mountain*

Luella Danielson
Pleasure Iris Gardens
425 East Luna
Chaparral, New Mexico 88021
telephone 505.824.4299
(1 May to 19 May)

Denver Botanic Gardens
909 York Street
Denver, Colorado 80206
telephone 303.331.4000
(20 May to 10 June)

Bob Dunkley
Mountain View Garden
2435 Middle Road
Columbia Falls, Montana 59912
telephone 406.982.5020
(10 June to 1 August)*

Harry B. Kuesel
Old Brook Gardens
4 Larkdale Drive
Littleton, Colorado 80123
telephone 303.795.9718
(30 May to 20 June)

Morris Steinheimer
7 McBurney Boulevard
Colorado Springs, Colorado
    80911
telephone 719.392.7580
(30 May to 30 June)

• *West Coast*

Terry Aitken
Aitken's Salmon Creek Garden
608 NW 119th Street
Vancouver, Washington 98685
telephone 206.573.4472
(10 May to 10 June)*

Chehalem Gardens
P.O. Box 693
Newberg, Oregon 97132
(late May to mid-June)

Carla M. Lankow
11118 169th Avenue SE
Renton, Washington 98056
(20 May to late June)

Maxwelton Valley Gardens
3443 East French Road
Clinton, Washington 98236
telephone 206.579.1770
(5 May to 30 June)

Lorena M. Reid
Laurie's Garden
41886 McKenzie Highway
Springfield, Oregon 97478
telephone 503.896.3756
(May to late June)

Dorothy and Allan Rogers
Caprice Farm Nursery
15425 SW Pleasant Hill Road
Sherwood, Oregon 97140
telephone 503.625.7241
(late May to mid-June)

Nancy and David Silverberg
Abbey Gardens
32009 South Ona Way
Molalla, Oregon 97038
telephone 503.829.2928
(15 May to 15 June)

Jean G. Witt
16516 25th NE
Seattle, Washington 98155
telephone 206.362.9206
(20 May to 20 June)*

Australia

Lesley and Barry Blyth
Tempo Two
P.O. Box 60A
Pearcedale, Victoria
telephone 059.78.6980
(1 November to mid-December)

Helen and Graeme Grosvenor,
  John Taylor
Rainbow Ridge Nursery
Taylor Road
Dural, New South Wales 2158
telephone 02.651.2857
(late October to late November)

Belgium

Koen Engelen
Kawana
Wijnegembaan
2520 Ranst
telephone 03.35402
(25 May to 31 June)

Alphonse Van Mulders
Rue du Plangelois 17
5210 Javiers
telephone 081.812271
(mid-May to late June)

Britain

The Beth Chatto Gardens Ltd
Elmstead Market
Colchester
Essex CO7 7DB
telephone 01206.822007
(late May to late June)

John Carter
Rowden Gardens
Brentor near Tavistock
Devon PL19 0NG
telephone 01822.810275
(1 June to 30 June)*

Croftway Nursery
Yapton Road
Barnham near Rognor Regis
West Sussex PO22 0BH
telephone 01243.552121
(15 May to late June)

David Austin Roses
Bowling Green Lane
Albrighton, Wolverhampton
West Midlands WV7 3HB
telephone 01902.373931
(early June to late June)

Kim W. Davis
Lingen Alpine Nursery
Lingen near Bucknell
Shropshire SY7 0DY
telephone 01554.267720
(early June to late June)

David Dixon
Walnut Cottage
3 Newark Drive
Whitburn
Sunderland SR3 7DF
telephone 01915.293058
(late May to late June)*

Four Seasons
Forncett St. Mary
Norwich
Norfolk NR16 1JT
telephone 01508.488344
(early June to late June)

Jennifer Hewitt
Haygarth
Cleeton St. Mary
Cleobury Mortimer
Kidderminster DY14 0QU
telephone 01584.890526
(1 June to 30 June)*

Holden Clough Nursery
Holden
Bolton-by-Bowland
Clitheroe
Lancashire BB7 4PF
telephone 01200.447615
(early June to late June)

V. H. Humphrey
Westlees Farm, Logmore Lane
Westcott, Dorking
Surrey RH4 3JN
telephone 01306.889827
(mid-May to 30 June)

Perryhill Nursery
Harfield
East Sussex TN7 4JP
telephone 01892.770377
(mid-May to late June)

J. A. Smart
Marwood Hill Gardens
Barnstaple
North Devon EX31 4EB
telephone 01271.42528
(mid-May to mid-June)

The Water Garden Nursery
Highcroft, Moorend
Wembworthy, Chulmeigh
Devon EX18 7SG
telephone 01837.83566
(mid-May to mid-June)

Canada

Catherine Boyko
Route 9, Bains Road
Dunnville, Ontario N1A 2W8
telephone 905.774.8360
(early June to late June)

Les Jardins Osiris
818 Rue Monique
St. Thomas de Joliette,
    Quebec J0K 3L0
telephone 514.759.8621
(early June to late June)

Verna Laurin
199 Florence Avenue
Willowdale, Ontario M2N 1G5
telephone 416.225.1088
(early June to late June)

Gloria McMillen
McMillen's Iris Garden
Route 1
Norwich, Ontario N0J 1P0
telephone 519.468.6508
(early June to late June)

Royal Botanical Gardens
P.O. Box 399
Hamilton, Ontario L8N 3H8
telephone 905.527.1158
(early June to late June)

Irene Specogna
15163 Humber Station Road
Bolton, Ontario L7E 5S1
telephone 905.880.4461
(late June to mid-July)

France

Bourdillon Nursery
Gaec de Champagne
41230 Soings-en-Sologne
(mid-May to mid-June)

Richard Cayeux
Cayeux Nursery
Poilly-lez-Gien
45500 Gien
(mid-May to mid-June)

Germany

Friesland Staudengarten
Uwe Knöpnadel
Husumer Weg 16
26441 Jever-Rahdum
(May to June)

Schöppinger Irisgarten
Bürgerweg 8
48624 Schoppingen
(early June to late June)

Eberhard Schuster
Post Gaedebehn
19089 Augustenhof
(early June to late June)

Tomas Tamberg
Zimmerstrasse 8
12207 Berlin
telephone 030.712.4235
(1 June to 15 June)*

New Zealand

Bay Bloom Nursery
Box 502
Tauranga
(7 November to early December)

Mossburn Iris Gardens
Box 96, Private Bag
Mossburn, Southland
(late November to mid-December)

Ranch North Iris Gardens
RD 3
Whangarei
(7 November to early December)

Appendix C

Sources
of Plants
and Equipment

Visitors to many of the gardens listed in Appendix B can obtain siberian irises at the time of their visits. The sources listed in this appendix are limited to those that have a catalog and can sell on a mail-order basis.

This list certainly is incomplete, especially on the international front. I apologize to those that I have failed to include.

Sources of Plants

United States

Abbey Gardens
Nancy and David Silverberg
32009 South Ona Way
Molalla, Oregon 97038
own introductions and general list

Aitken's Salmon Creek Garden
Terry Aitken
608 NW 119th Street
Vancouver, Washington 98685
own introductions and general list

Amberway Gardens
5803 Amberway Drive
St. Louis, Missouri 63128
general list

Louise Bellagamba
11431 Old Saint Charles Road
Bridgeton, Missouri 63044-3075
own introductions and general list

Borbeleta Gardens
Julius Wadekamper
15980 Canby Avenue
Faribault, Minnesota 55021
own introductions and general list

Borglum Irises
Dana Borglum
2202 Austin Road
Geneva, New York 14456
own introductions and general list

Bush Gardens
George C. Bush
1739 Memory Lane Extd
York, Pennsylvania 17402
own introductions and general list

Busse Gardens Co., Inc.
Ainie Busse
5873 Oliver Avenue SW
Cokato, Minnesota 55321
own introductions and general list

Caprice Farm Nursery
Dorothy and Allan Rogers
15425 SW Pleasant Hill Road
Sherwood, Oregon 97140
general list

Chehalem Gardens
P.O. Box 693
Newberg, Oregon 97132
general list

Coopers Garden
Penny Aquirre
2345 Decatur Avenue North
Golden Valley, Minnesota 55427
general list

Draycott Gardens
Carol Warner
16815 Falls Road
Upperco, Maryland 21155
general list

Eartheart Gardens
Sharon Hayes Whitney
RR 1, Box 847
South Harpswell, Maine 04079
McEwen introductions

James L. Ennenga
1621 North 85th Street
Omaha, Nebraska 68114
own introductions and general list

Ensata Gardens
Robert Bauer and John Coble
9823 East Michigan Avenue
Galesburg, Michigan 49053
own introductions and general list

Fieldstone Gardens, Inc.
Steven D. Jones
620 Quaker Lane
Vassalboro, Maine 04985-9713
McEwen introductions

Dale Hamblin
152 North Idlewild
Mundelein, Illinois 60060
general list

Larry L. Harder
208 First Street
Ponca, Nebraska 68770
general list

Heschke Gardens
David Heschke
11503 77th Street South
Hastings, Minnesota 55033
general list

Illini Iris
Steve Varner
Route 3, Box 5
Monticello, Illinois 61856
own introductions and general list

Sterling Innerst
2700-A Oakland Road
Dover, Pennsylvania 17315
general list

The Iris Pond
Suky and Clarence Mahan
7311 Churchill Road
McLean, Virginia 22101
own introductions and general list

Joe Pye Weed's Garden
Janet Sacks and Martin Schafer
337 Acton Street
Carlisle, Massachusetts 01741
own introductions and general list

Klehm Nursery of Champaign
Kit and Roy Klehm
4210 North Duncan Road
Champaign, Illinois 61821
own introductions and general list

Laurie's Garden
Lorena M. Reid
41886 McKenzie Highway
Springfield, Oregon 97478
own introductions and general list

Mid-America Garden
3409 North Geraldine
Oklahoma City, Oklahoma
    73112-2806
general list

Miller's Manor Gardens
3167 Route 224
Ossian, Indiana 46777
general list

Mountain View Garden
Bob Dunkley
2435 Middle Road
Columbia Falls, Montana 59912
general list

Nicholls Gardens
Diana and Mike Nicholls
4724 Angus Drive
Gainesville, Virginia 22065
general list

Old Brook Gardens
Harry B. Kuesel
4 Larkdale Drive
Littleton, Colorado 80123
own introductions and general list

Old Douglas Perennials
Anna Mae and Ronald Miller
6065 North 16th Street
Kalamazoo, Michigan 49007
own introductions and general list

Phoenix Gardens
Kevin J. Morley
8404 Cherry
Kansas City, Missouri 64131
own introductions and general list

Pine Ridge Gardens
Route 1, Box 474-IRIS
London, Arkansas 72847
general list

Pleasure Iris Gardens
Luella Danielson
425 East Luna
Chaparral, New Mexico 88021
general list

Pope's Perennials
Shirley L. Pope
39 Highland Avenue
Gorham, Maine 04038-1701
general list

Quail Hill Gardens
Everette Lineberger
2460 Compton Bridge Road
Inman, South Carolina
  29349-8489
general list

Redbud Lane Iris Garden
Melody and Jerry Wilhoit
Route 1, Box 141
Kansas, Illinois 61933
general list

Harold L. Stahly
8343 Manchester Drive
Grand Blanc, Michigan 48439
own introductions

Stephens Lane Gardens
Route 1, Box 136-H
Bells, Tennessee 38006
general list

Thistle Ridge Gardens
RR 1, Box 625
Spencer, Indiana 47460
general list

Tranquil Lake Nursery, Inc.
Philip Boucher
45 River Street
Rehoboth, Massachusetts 02769
general list

Valente Gardens
Cindy and Ron Valente
RFD 2, Box 234
East Lebanon, Maine 04027
general list

Walnut Hill Gardens
Lynn and Barrett Stoll
999 310th Street
Atalissa, Iowa 52720
general list

White Flower Farm
Route 63
Litchfield, Connecticut 06759
general list

Windwood Gardens
Judith and Robert Hollingworth
124 Sherwood Road East
Williamston, Michigan 48895
own introductions

John W. Wood
2654 Prospect Church Road
Mooresboro, North Carolina
  28114
own introductions and general list

York Hill Farm
Darlyn C. Springer
18 Warren Street
Georgetown, Massachusetts 01833
general list

Australia

Rainbow Ridge Nursery
Helen and Graeme Grosvenor,
    John Taylor
Taylor Road
Dural, New South Wales 2158
telephone 02.651.2857
general list

Tempo Two
Lesley and Barry Blyth
P.O. Box 60A
Pearcedale, Victoria
telephone 059.78.6980
own introductions and general list

Belgium

Koen Engelen
Kawana
Wijnegembaan
2520 Ranst
telephone 03.35402
general list

Alphonse Van Mulders
Rue du Plangelois 17
5210 Javiers
telephone 081.812271
general list

Britain

The Beth Chatto Gardens Ltd
Elmstead Market
Colchester
Essex CO7 7DB
telephone 01206.822007
general list

Croftway Nursery
Yapton Road
Barnham near Rognor Regis
West Sussex PO22 0BH
telephone 01243.552121
general list

David Austin Roses
Bowling Green Lane
Albrighton, Wolverhampton
West Midlands WV7 3HB
telephone 01902.373931
general list

Four Seasons
Forncett St. Mary
Norwich
Norfolk NR16 1JT
telephone 01508.488344
general list

Jennifer Hewitt
Haygarth
Cleeton St. Mary
Cleobury Mortimer
Kidderminster DY14 0QU
telephone 01584.890526
own introductions and general list

Holden Clough Nursery
Holden
Bolton-by-Bowland
Clitheroe
Lancashire BB7 4PF
telephone 01200.447615
general list

V. H. Humphrey
Westlees Farm, Logmore Lane
Westcott, Dorking
Surrey RH4 3JN
telephone 01306.889827
general list

Lingen Alpine Nursery
Kim W. Davis
Lingen near Bucknell
Shropshire SY7 0DY
telephone 01554.267720
general list

Perryhill Nursery
Harfield
East Sussex TN7 4JP
telephone 01892.770377
general list

Rowden Gardens
John Carter
Brentor near Tavistock
Devon PL19 0NG
telephone 01822.810275
general list

The Water Garden Nursery
Highcroft, Moorend
Wembworthy, Chulmeigh
Devon EX18 7SG
telephone 01837.83566
general list

Canada

Les Jardins Osiris
818 Rue Monique
St. Thomas de Joliette,
    Quebec J0K 3L0
telephone 514.759.8621
general list

Gloria McMillen
McMillen's Iris Garden
Route 1
Norwich, Ontario N0J 1P0
general list

France

Bourdillon Nursery
Gaec de Champagne
41230 Soings-en-Sologne
general list

Cayeux Nursery
Richard Cayeux
Poilly-lez-Gien
45500 Gien
general list

Germany

Friesland Staudengarten
Uwe Knöpnadel
Husumer Weg 16
26441 Jever-Rahdum
own introductions and general list

Schöppinger Irisgarten
Bürgerweg 8
48624 Schoppingen
general list

Eberhard Schuster
Post Gaedebehn
19089 Augustenhof
general list

Tomas Tamberg
Zimmerstrasse 8
12207 Berlin
telephone 030.712.4235
own introductions and general list

New Zealand

Bay Bloom Nursery
Box 502
Tauranga
general list

Mossburn Iris Gardens
Box 96, Private Bag
Mossburn, Southland
general list

Ranch North Iris Gardens
RD 3
Whangarei
general list

Sources of Equipment

Gardener's Supply Company
128 Intervale Road
Burlington, Vermont 05401-2850
for accelerated propagation system

Growing Systems, Inc.
2950 North Weil Street
Milwaukee, Wisconsin 53212
for groove tubes

Appendix D

Tetraploidy: Methods and Identification

The nature of tetraploidy is discussed in Chapter 2. This appendix is devoted to methods for inducing tetraploidy and to its identification.

Methods for Inducing Tetraploidy

Tetraploidy is usually induced in one of two simple ways: one involves a fairly mature plant (referred to as the clonal method), and the other, newly sprouted seedlings. More complex methods, requiring embryo culture and tissue culture, are also practiced, but these complicated laboratory procedures are not presented here; for detailed information on one way of using embryo culture, the interested reader is referred to Yabuya (1985).

Colchicine, the chemical substance that induces polyploidy, figures in all methods; it may be helpful, therefore, to briefly describe colchicine's mode of action. Mitosis is a process of cell division which leads to the normal growth of plants. During mitosis, at a stage known as metaphase, the chromosomes double, forming two sets that then move to opposite sides of the cell. This movement is caused by a transient structure called the spindle, the infinitely fine strands of which draw the two sets of doubled chromosomes to opposite sides of the cell in preparation for division. Colchicine temporarily inhibits the spindle's critical action, halting mitosis. When the effect of the colchicine wears off, mitosis starts again. In most cells, growth resumes in the normal diploid fashion, but in some, the chromosomes double a second time, with each of the resulting daughter cells thus in possession of twice the usual diploid number.

Since colchicine induces polyploidy by its ability to temporarily paralyze the spindle's action, other substances affecting the spindle in the same way should presumably induce polyploidy also. Several herbicides are among the chemical substances that act as spindle poisons; trifluralin is perhaps the best known. Kevin Vaughn of the United States Department of Agriculture Weed Science Laboratory in Stoneville, Mississippi, has used trifluralin successfully to induce polyploidy in louisiana irises (Vaughn 1991), but no trials of its use in siberian irises have yet been reported.

Clonal method

Arisumi (1964), working with daylilies, described the standard clonal method. A plant stem, approximately 0.5 inch (1 centimeter) in diameter, is cut off about 0.5 inch (1 centimeter) above the meristem at the crown, and a cuplike depression about 0.25 inch (6 millimeters) deep is scooped into the stump. This hollow is filled with a 0.5-percent aqueous solution of colchicine every other day for three treatments. Like Arisumi, I have used this method successfully with daylilies, but my trials with siberian irises have failed. In them, I used a series of strengths of colchicine, from 0.025 to 0.5 percent. All treated plants were either killed or remained diploid.

Norris (1991), working with louisiana irises, successfully modified the method by not cutting off the plant and by using a disposable hypodermic syringe to inject 0.15 to 0.25 milliliters of a 0.4-percent colchicine solution into the plant just above the meristem. This modification has not yet been tried with siberians.

Sprouted seedling method

I have used with great success what I think of as the standard method, developed by Robert Griesbach and Orville Fay in their work with daylilies (Griesbach et al 1963; McEwen 1966). Note: All steps prior to the colchicine treatment must be carried out with sterilized equipment and water.

Collect the seeds when ripe. Before storing them in the usual way, carefully inspect the seeds and discard any that show suspicion of mold or that appear to be empty and nonviable. As an additional measure, dust the seeds very lightly with the fungicide thiram before placing them in plastic sandwich bags. Finally, add one to ten drops of sterile water, depending on the number of seeds, before sealing the packets. The seeds are not sterile, of course, but should be made as free as possible of infectious agents.

When the time arrives to start the colchicine treatment, place the seeds in sterile bacteriological plates (petri dishes) on moist filter or blotting paper that has been sterilized by heating at 200 degrees Fahrenheit (93 degrees Celsius) for an hour. Keep the dishes, properly labeled as to which particular seeds they contain, at 70 to 75 degrees Fahrenheit (21 to 24 degrees Celsius).

In a few weeks the seeds sprout. First the small white hypocotyl appears; in another day or two, the primitive root starts growing from the end of the hypocotyl, and a small slit develops on the hypocotyl's side. In another few days, the green of new leaves can be seen in the slit. I treat the seeds when the tiny green shoots are 0.03 to 0.10 inch (1 to 3 millimeters) in size. Each night, remove the seedlings that have attained this size and place them in a test tube of colchicine solution; each cross should be kept in a separate, labeled tube. The seeds removed need no longer be treated aseptically, but they should be taken out of the petri dishes with a flamed forceps so as not to infect the remaining seeds.

Colchicine solutions for treating the sprouted seedling are much weaker than those used for the clonal method, usually from 0.025 to 0.05 percent. Place the tubes with the seeds in the colchicine under lights for twelve hours overnight. In the morning, save the colchicine for the next use and wash the sprouted seedlings for one or two hours with three changes of water. Plant the seedlings in growing mix under lights at approximately 70 degrees Fahrenheit (21 degrees Celsius). In a week or so, the polyploid seedlings can be distinguished from their diploid siblings because they remain stubby and small, whereas the diploid ones grow rapidly in the usual manner.

The sad part comes approximately three weeks later, when many of the obviously affected seedlings begin to die. In the primitive root of all affected seedlings, one will find a small, tumorlike enlargement. I have examined stained histologic sections of these growths with the microscope and have found them to be masses of cells growing in disorganized fashion, rendering all nutrient channels so blocked that the primitive root is useless. I believe that the fate of the seedlings depends on the development of the secondary roots from the hypocotyl. If they grow before the endosperm is spent, the seedling lives. If not, the seedling starves. For a month or more, the surviving polyploid seedlings grow slowly, but then they start growing well and in a few more weeks are often similar to the diploid ones.

In my experience using this method, perhaps 50 to 80 percent of the treated seedlings die, and of those that survive, 5 to 40 percent are polyploid. Rarely one may be fully tetraploid, but more commonly they are chimeras, which may, in time, revert to the diploid state. Crossing two chimeras will result in either diploids or full tetraploids, depending largely on the degree of polyploidy of the parents, but no further chimeras issue from such a cross.

Over the years since this original method was described, it has been modified by several hybridizers. Robert Hollingworth's variation is as follows. Instead of petri dishes, he uses small glass jars, such as baby food jars. The seeds, which have been stored in the refrigerator over winter in the dry state, are placed in the jars for five or six hours in hypochlorite bleach (one part bleach to five parts water). The jars are occasionally shaken, and the seeds are rinsed several times over three to four days in their jars with cooled, boiled water, which is then poured off, leaving only the water retained by the seeds. Fungal infections before germination are treated by soaking seeds for a few hours in a small amount of benomyl suspended in water, followed by a sterile water wash.

The closed jars are kept at 70 to 75 degrees Fahrenheit (21 to 24 degrees Celsius). Occasional bottom heat to 80 degrees Fahrenheit (26 degrees Celsius) helps germination in some cases. When the germinating seeds have reached the stage suitable for treatment (as in the standard method), they are soaked in a colchicine solution (0.035 to 0.045 percent) for approximately eight hours. They are then washed in water for a few hours with three changes of water and are left in their jars in the moist state.

About two weeks later, they are planted in flats in a germinating mix. By that time, the character of growth gives a fairly accurate impression of whether the individual seedlings have been affected by the colchicine; hence, those apparently affected and those not can be planted separately or, if space is a problem, only the ones that appear to be affected need be planted. The colchicine concentration can be adjusted in later batches to achieve the desired percent affected (70 to 80 percent).

Identification of Tetraploids

The hybridizer can gain a fair impression as to whether a treated seedling is diploid or polyploid merely from its appearance. In the polyploid, leaves and stalks are larger than in the diploids, and their color is a deeper green. The flowers are larger and have firmer substance (Figure 2-2), and their colors tend to be richer.

Examination of the anthers is still more conclusive, as polyploid anthers are much larger than those on diploid flowers, but the definitive test is to examine the pollen grains under a microscope. Pollen grains of tetraploids are nearly twice as large as those of diploids. The procedure is simple and takes only a few minutes. One merely dusts a small amount of pollen from an anther into a drop of water on a glass slide and examines it. Even a very simple microscope will do, since even a tenfold magnification suffices. Under the microscope, the grains actually appear less than twice the diploid size because they are seen in only two dimensions, but they still look distinctly larger; having a measuring glass (reticle) in the eyepiece of the microscope makes the comparison of sizes easier and more exact.

The size of pollen grains from colchicine-treated plants tells not only whether polyploidy has been achieved but also the degree of polyploidy. The growing point of the plant, the meristem, is cone-shaped (with the pointed end up) and made up of three layers. The outer layer, layer one, gives rise to the ectoderm (the "skin" of the plant) and about one sixth of the reproductive cells. The layer beneath it, layer two, gives rise to the rest of the reproductive cells and contributes in a minor way to the flower components, leaves, and stalks. Although not strictly a layer, the cells that fill the base of the meristem under layer two are known as layer three. From them come the "bone and muscle" of the plant—the leaves, stalks, flowers, rhizome, and roots—but they contribute nothing to the reproductive cells. If one finds upon microscopic examination of a treated plant's pollen grains that most are diploid, with only a few of tetraploid size, the part of the plant that carries the flower from which the pollen came is tetraploid in layer one and diploid in layer two, or what is known as a 4-2 chimera. If most of the pollen grains are tetraploid and only a few are diploid, that part of the plant is a 2-4 chimera. If all pollen grains are small, that part of the plant is diploid. If all the grains are tetraploid, that part of the plant is fully tetraploid in both layers one and two, abbreviated as a 4-4. Examination of the pollen gives no information about layer three, of course.

From the standpoint of a particular plant's usefulness for tetraploid breeding, a plant that is fully tetraploid is, of course, ideal—but that is rare. Fortunately, a 2-4 chimera is very nearly as useful as a fully tetraploid one for tetraploid breeding. Crossed with a tetraploid, it yields only tetraploid seedlings. Crossed with another 2-4 chimera, the chances are good that resulting seedlings will be fully tetraploid. Even crossed with a 4-2 chimera, a tetraploid seedling may result, but in all probability all will be diploids.

One naturally thinks of taking a chromosome count to determine whether a plant is diploid or tetraploid. This can indeed be useful in the study of plants that one believes may have reached the second or a later generation of tetraploidy, but a chromosome count is not only unnecessary but can be misleading in the study of colchicine-treated seedlings. Chromosome counts are usually done on root tips, but the roots yield no information concerning the ploidy of layers one and two, from which the reproductive cells arise. In a test seedling, layer two might be tetraploid, but the chromosome count of the root tips may be diploid, leading a breeder working for tetraploids to discard a useful seedling.

Remember that even a useful 2-4 chimera can in time revert to diploid form. Hence, unless there is some important reason for introducing a colchicine-treated cultivar as polyploid, the breeder had best wait until the second generation of tetraploidy has been reached. Only at that point can a breeder be confident that a seedling is fully tetraploid.

References

Abrego, T. 1993. Personal communication.

Ahrens, E. H., Jr. 1994. Personal communication.

Aitken, T. 1994. Personal communication.

American Iris Society. 1959. L. F. Randolph, ed. *Garden Irises*. St. Louis, Missouri: American Iris Society.

———. 1978. B. Warburton and M. Hamblen, eds. *The World of Irises*. Wichita, Kansas: American Iris Society.

———. 1985. P. A. Williams, ed. *Handbook for Judges and Show Officials*. 5th ed. Tulsa, Oklahoma: American Iris Society.

———. 1992. K. Nelson, ed. *Iris Check List of Registered Cultivar Names 1980–1989*. Tulsa, Oklahoma: American Iris Society.

———. 1994. K. Nelson-Keppel, ed. *Registrations and Introductions in 1993*. Tulsa, Oklahoma: American Iris Society.

Arisumi, T. 1964. Colchicine-induced tetraploid and cytochimeral daylilies. *Journal of Heredity* 5:254–261; reprint 1966, *Hemerocallis Journal* 20:59–67.

Bald, J. G. 1969. Scorch disease of rhizomatous irises. *Bulletin of the American Iris Society* No. 195:26–30.

Barnett, O. W. 1972. Viruses of irises. *Bulletin of the American Iris Society* No. 205:27–31.

Baruch, E., and F. Quak. 1966. Virus free plants of *Iris* 'Wedgewood' obtained by meristem culture. *Netherlands Journal of Plant Pathology* 71:270–273.

Bauer, R. A., and J. A. Coble. 1994. Personal communication.

Berlin, E. 1989. A new iris for very cold climates. *The Siberian Iris* 6(9): 12–14.

Brickell, C. D., ed. 1980. *International Code of Nomenclature for Culti-vated Plants*. Utrecht: International Bureau for Plant Taxonomy and Nomenclature.

Burton, V. 1993. Personal communication.

Coble, J. A. 1987. From pollination to bloom in two years. *Bulletin of the American Iris Society* No. 266:39–40.

Cowan, J. M. 1952. *The Journeys and Plant Introductions of George Forrest V.M.H.* London: Oxford University Press.

Davidson, B. L. 1974. Notes on the *Sibiricae* material at Kent. *The Siberian Iris* 3(10): 15–16.

——. 1977. Two scraps of information on *I. phragmitetorum*. *The Siberian Iris* 4(5): 20.

——. 1982. The clouded *Iris bulleyana*. *The Siberian Iris* 5(6): 4–6.

——. 1989. Siberian irises in cultivation: a history. *Bulletin of the American Iris Society* No. 274:9–12.

——. 1992. Personal communication.

Deno, N. C. 1994. *Seed Germination Theory and Practice*. Self-published, 139 Lenor Drive, State College, Pennsylvania 16801.

Dimock, A. W. 1959. Diseases of rhizomatous iris. In *Garden Irises*, L. F. Randolph, ed., 108–109. St. Louis, Missouri: American Iris Society.

Dykes, W. R. 1913. *The Genus Iris*. Cambridge: Cambridge University Press; reprint 1974, New York: Dover Publications.

Edwards, P. 1959. The Siberian situation. *Bulletin of the American Iris Society* No. 154:65–69.

Eigsti, O. J., and P. Dustin, Jr. 1955. *Colchicine in Agriculture, Medicine, Biology and Chemistry*. Ames: Iowa State College Press.

Grey, C. H. 1938. *Hardy Bulbs*. New York: E. P. Dutton and Co.

Grey-Wilson, C. 1971. *The Genus Iris Subsection Sibiricae*. London: British Iris Society.

Griesbach, R. Z., O. W. Fay, and L. Horsfall. 1963. Induction of polyploidy in newly germinated hemerocallis seedlings. *Hemerocallis Journal* 17:70–75.

Hager, B. R. 1987. Japanese iris culture and problems. *Bulletin of the American Iris Society* No. 266:42–44.

——. 1992. Personal communication.

Hansford, D. 1968. Some new hybrid sibiricas. In *The Iris Year Book 1968*, 106–108. London: British Iris Society.

Heinig, K. 1959. Check list of iris species hybrids. In *Garden Irises*, L. F. Randolph, ed., 516–536. St. Louis, Missouri: American Iris Society.

Helsley, C. 1983. Those forty-chromosome siberians. *The Siberian Iris* 5(8): 67.

Hewitt, J. 1990. The fascinating forties. *The Siberian Iris* 7(1): 20–25.

Hirao, S. 1984. The Japanese iris in Japan. *The Review* 21(1): 11–13.

Hoebeke, E. R. 1994a. Some flies associated with irises. *Cornell Plantation* 49(3): 12–14.

———. 1994b. Personal communication.

Hoitink, H. A. J., and M. E. Grebus. 1994. Status of biological control of plant diseases with composts. *Compost Science and Utilization* 2(2): 6–12.

Hollingworth, J. 1987. A gardener's scourge. *The Siberian Iris* 6(5): 8.

———. 1988. Moles: the final chapter. *The Siberian Iris* 6(8): 27–28.

Hollingworth, R. M. 1979. Botrytis rot of siberian irises. *The Siberian Iris* 4(9): 12–14.

———. 1985. Siberian disease identified. *The Siberian Iris* 6(1): 20–22.

———. 1991. A note regarding triacontanol. *The Siberian Iris* 7(3): 8–9.

———. 1994. Personal communication.

Horinaka, A. 1992. *Iris sanguinea* down in Japan. *The Siberian Iris* 7(6): 22–23.1987.

———. 1994. Personal communication.

Ichie, T. 1991. Personal communication.

Ito, T. 1966. The culture of irises in Japan. *The Review* 1(3): 36–35.

Kamo, M. 1989. Personal communication.

Kitagawa, M. 1939. Key to northeast plants. In *Lineamenta Florae Manshuricae*. Report of the Institute of Scientific Research, Manchoukuo, Vol. 3, Appendix 1:1–488.

———. 1979. *Neo-Lineamenta Florae Manshuricae*. Vaduz, Liechtenstein: Cramer.

Kondratas, E. 1994. Personal communication.

Korcak, R. F. 1987. Iron deficiency chlorosis. In Vol. 9, *Horticultural Reviews*, J. Janick, ed., 133–186. Portland, Oregon: Timber Press.

———. 1992. Short term responses of blueberry to elevated soil calcium. *Journal of Small Fruit and Viticulture* 1(2): 9–21.

Lawrence, G. H. M. 1953. A reclassification of the genus *Iris*. *Gentes Herbarium* 8:346–371.

Lenz, L. 1959. Two new and unusual iris hybrids. *Bulletin of the American Iris Society* No. 144:43–46.

———. 1976. A reclassification of the siberian iris. *Aliso* 8(4): 379–338; reprint 1977, *The Siberian Iris* 4(5): 4-6.

Loveridge, G. B. 1988. Personal communication.

Luihn, V. 1973. California commentary I. cultural reflections. *The Siberian Iris* 3(8): 9–11.

Malloch, J. R. 1924. New and little known calyptrate diptera from New England. *Psyche* 31:193–205.

Markham, L. F. 1994. Personal communication.

Mathew, B. 1990. *The Iris*. Portland, Oregon: Timber Press.

McEwen, C. 1966. Tetraploidy in siberian irises. In *The Iris Year Book 1966*, 77–84. London: British Iris Society.

——. 1971a. A note on the 40-chromosome siberians. *The Siberian Iris* 3(3): 3–7.

——. 1971b. Obtaining early maturity of seedlings in the north. *Bulletin of the American Iris Society* No. 203:65–66.

——. 1973. Factors influencing germination of japanese iris seeds and health of the sprouted seedlings. *The Review* 10(2): 4–6.

——. 1974a. Observations regarding siberian irises in Europe 1974. *The Siberian Iris* 3(10): 5–7.

——. 1974b. Nomenclature of siberian irises. *The Siberian Iris* 3(10): 11–14.

——. 1974c. Factors influencing the germination of japanese iris seeds. *Bulletin of the American Iris Society* No. 213:32–36.

——. 1976. Historical note on hybridizing of siberian irises. *The Siberian Iris* 4(3): 8–14.

——. 1977. Final report of the ad hoc committee on nomenclature. *The Siberian Iris* 4(5): 7–9.

——. 1978a. Experience with *Pratylenchus penetrans*. *The Siberian Iris* 4(8): 8–10.

——. 1978b. A note about the small ones. *The Siberian Iris* 4(8): 16–18.

——. 1979. Experience with rebloom in siberian and japanese irises. *Bulletin of the American Iris Society* No. 233:73–77.

——. 1983. A choice of terms for remontancy in siberian and japanese irises. *The Siberian Iris* 5(7): 8–9.

——. 1987. 'Butter and Sugar': its background. *The Siberian Iris* 6(5): 5–6.

——. 1991. Japanese iris culture in Japan. *The Review* 22(2): 38–42.

McEwen, C., and B. Warburton. 1971. Report of a research project to test various methods of making crosses of siberian irises. *The Siberian Iris* 3(4): 19–22.

McGarvey, W. G. 1975. The culture and hybridizing of siberian irises: a short history and report of current work. *Bulletin of the American Iris Society* No. 219:20–27.

Meyer, M. M., L. H. Fuchigami, and A. N. Roberts. 1975. Propagation of tall bearded irises by tissue culture. *Hort. Science* 10(5): 479–480.

Meyer, P., J. Heidmann, G. Forkmann, and H. Saedler. 1987. A new petunia flower color generated by transformation of a mutant with a maize gene. *Nature* 330:677–678.

Miller, A. M. 1990. Floral design with siberian irises. *The Siberian Iris* 7(1): 16–19.

Naegele, J. A. 1959. Insect pests of irises. In *Garden Irises*, L. F. Randolph, ed., 121. St. Louis, Missouri: American Iris Society.

Norris, S. N. 1991. Colchicine-induced polyploidy. *SLI Newsletter* (Society for Louisiana Irises) 146: 6–8.

Pope, S. 1988. Siberian iris culture. *The Siberian Iris*. 6(7): 13.

Randolph, L. F. 1959. Embryo culture of iris seeds. In *Garden Irises*, L. F. Randolph, ed., 87–92. St. Louis, Missouri: American Iris Society.

Reid, L. 1991. Hybridizing sino-siberian irises in the northwest. *The Siberian Iris* 7(3): 12–16.

Rodionenko, G. I. 1961. *The Genus Iris L.* Leningrad: Academy of Sciences of the USSR, V. L. Domarov Botanical Institute. Translated 1984 by T. A. Blanco White for the British Iris Society; published 1987, London: British Iris Society.

———. 1964. Wild iris species of the USSR. In *The Iris Year Book 1964*, 117–119. London: British Iris Society.

———. 1992. Improving iris adaptability for northern regions. In *The Iris Year Book 1992*, 70–72. London: British Iris Society.

Schafer, M. 1989. New thoughts on pollination. *The Siberian Iris* 6(9): 5–6.

———. 1994. Personal communication.

Shidara, H. 1992. Breeding of 'Yaezaki-ayame'. *The Siberian Iris* 7(5): 17–18.

Shimizu, H. 1992. Development of siberian irises in Japan. *The Siberian Iris* 7(5): 21–22.

Simonet, M. 1934. Nouvelles recherches cytologiques et génétiques chez les iris. *Ann. Sci. Nat. Bot*, Series 10, 15:229–383.

———. 1951. Sur la méiose de quelques hybrides d'iris apogon: I. hybrides *Sibiricae, Californicae* et *Setosae. Compt. Rend. Hebd. Seances Acad. Sci.* 233:1665–1667.

Sjolund, R. 1993. Personal communication.

Sjolund, R., L. Stoll, and K. Jensen. 1990. Iris scorch disease. *American Iris Society Region 21 Bulletin* No. 107:36–39.

Smith, R. G. 1993. Transgenic modifications for irises. *Bulletin of the American Iris Society* No. 289:54–58.

Smith, R. H., and T. Murashige. 1970. In vitro development of the isolated shoot apical meristem of angiosperms. *American Journal of Botany* 57:562–568.

Society for Siberian Irises. 1991. *The 1991 Cumulative Check List of Siberian Irises,* H. L. Brookins, ed. Menomonee Falls, Wisconsin: Society for Siberian Irises.

Stark, G. 1974. Cultural reflections from the midwest. *The Siberian Iris* 3(9): 11–12.

Swanson, B. T., D. L. Newman, and J. B. Calkins. 1993. Weed control strategies for field grown herbaceous perennials 1990–1992. *The Siberian Iris* 7(8): 8–15.

Tamberg, T. 1980. Apogon notes from the Tamberg garden. In *The Iris Year Book 1980,* 75–78. London: British Iris Society.

———. 1990. Approaches to hybridizing. In *The Iris Year Book 1990,* 73–76. London: British Iris Society.

———. 1992. New beardless hybrids: a progress report. In *The Iris Year Book 1992,* 77–82. London: British Iris Society.

———. 1994. Personal communication.

Tiffney, S. 1971. Notes on hybridizing siberians. *The Siberian Iris* 3(4): 6–12.

———. 1978. A new minor pest and what to do about it. *The Siberian Iris* 4(8): 5–8.

United States Department of Agriculture. 1960. *Index of Plant Diseases in the United States: Agricultural Handbook 165.* Washington, D.C.: U.S. Government Printing Office.

Varner, W. T. 1992. Feeding iris alfalfa pellets. *The Medianite* 33(2): 54–55.

Vaughn, K. 1978. Culture of various tissues. In *The World of Irises,* B. Warburton and M. Hamblen, eds., 429–430. Wichita, Kansas: American Iris Society.

———. 1991. Using herbicide treatment to induce tetraploidy in louisiana irises and comments on existing cultivars. *SLI Newsletter* (Society for Louisiana Irises) 146: 8–11.

Vogt, A. J. 1987. Personal communication.

Waddick, J. W. 1991. *Iris typhifolia*: the "new" siberian iris. *The Siberian Iris* 7(4): 14–16.

——. 1992. Searching for *Iris phragmitetorum*. *The Siberian Iris* 7(6): 6–8.

——. 1993. Personal communication.

Waddick, J. W., and Zhao Yu-tang. 1992. *Iris of China*. Portland, Oregon: Timber Press.

Wadekamper, J. 1972. Scorch in irises. *Bulletin of the American Iris Society* No. 204:21–23.

——. 1987. Siberian irises as cut flowers. *The Siberian Iris* 6(5): 4.

——. 1994. Personal communication.

Warner, C. 1992. Just try to fool mother nature. *Bulletin of the American Iris Society* No. 286:25–26.

Weiler, J. H. 1978. Diseases in irises. In *The World of Irises*, B. Warburton and M. Hamblen, eds., 343. Wichita, Kansas: American Iris Society.

Wise, B. 1990. *Iris typhifolia*. In *The Iris Year Book 1990*, 82. London: British Iris Society.

Witt, J. G. 1959. Interspecies hybrids. *Bulletin of the American Iris Society* No. 152:31.

——. 1971a. The 40-chromosome siberians. *The Siberian Iris* 3(4): 22–29.

——. 1971b. Cal-Sibes: a promising group of beardless iris hybrids. *Bulletin of the American Iris Society* No. 203:60–62.

——. 1978. Cal-Sibe hybrids. In *The World of Irises*, B. Warburton and M. Hamblen, eds., 225–231. Wichita, Kansas: American Iris Society.

——. 1992. What is this siberian? Several contributions. *Signa* 49:1797–1798.

——. 1993. Personal communication.

Yabuya, T. 1985. Amphidiploids between *Iris laevigata* Fisch. and *I. ensata* Thunb. induced through in vitro culture of embryos treated with colchicine. *Japan Journal of Breeding* 35:136–144.

Zimmermann, E. 1994. A slice of life: a gardener's guide to genetic engineering. *Minnesota Horticulturist* (February): 20–22.

Glossary

acid soil. Soil with an acid reaction, i.e., with pH lower than 7.0 (neutral), usually from 5.0 to 6.8. The lower the pH, the greater the acidity.

alkaline soil. Soil with an alkaline reaction, i.e., with pH above 7.0 (neutral). The higher the pH, the greater the alkalinity.

allopolyploid, or *alloploid*. A polyploid in which one or more sets of chromosomes come from different plants.

allotetraploid. A tetraploid that is alloploid.

aneuploid. A plant with cells that have one or more chromosomes more or less than the balanced diploid, triploid, tetraploid, or other polyploid number.

amoena (ah ME nut). An iris flower with white standards and colored falls.

amphidiploid. A hybrid between two plants that has at least one complete set of chromosomes derived from each parent plant.

anther. The pollen-bearing structure at the end of the stamen.

anthocyanin. The primary cell-sap pigment of iris flowers. The most common form in irises produces the blue-to-purple and red colors.

apogon (f<u>a</u>t <u>pope</u> <u>gon</u>dola). An iris without beard or crest.

aseptic. Without infection.

autopolyploid, or *autoploid*. A plant with cells that have more than two sets of homologous chromosomes.

backcross. The cross of a hybrid with either parent.

bicolor. A flower with standards and/or styles and falls of different colors.

bitone. A flower having standards and/or styles and falls of different shades of the same color.

blaze. See **signal**

bracts. Pointed, upright, leaflike structures growing from the stalk. They may be green, red, purple, or brown, and either fleshy or dry and papery (scarious). See also **spathes**

branch. An offshoot from the stalk bearing one or more flower buds at its end.

callus. A proliferating mass of undifferentiated tissue.

Calsibe. An interseries hybrid between the irises of series *Californicae* and the siberian irises of subseries *Chrysographes*.

capsule. See **seed pod**

chimera (<u>kite</u> MERE <u>ah</u>). A plant that is partly diploid and partly tetraploid; named for a monster in Greek mythology that was made up of several different animals.

chlorophyll. The green-colored substance in plants, necessary for photosynthesis.

chromosomes. Microscopic bodies within the nuclei of cells that contain the genes that control the hereditary characteristics of progeny. Their number is constant and characteristic for each species and cultivar. Somatic chromosomes are those of the somatic or general body cells and are twice the number of those in the reproductive cells, i.e., pollen and egg cells.

Chrysographes (crystal so GROg fees). The name of the subseries of the 40-chromosome siberian irises and of one of its species.

clone. A group of genetically identical individuals resulting from vegetative multiplication of a single plant.

colchicine (COLlar chicken scene). A substance (alkaloid) obtained from the autumn crocus (*Colchicum autumnale*), used in the treatment of gout and to induce chromosome doubling in plants.

continuing bloomer. A plant that sends up successive bloom stalks for an extended period of weeks without an intervening bloomless period.

crimped. Fine folds, or pleats, at the edges of falls and standards.

cross pollination, or *crossing*. Placing the pollen of one flower on the stigma of a genetically dissimilar flower to fertilize it.

cultivar. A group of genetically identical plants maintained in cultivation for ornamental or utilitarian purposes. They are most often identified with names in a modern language, such as 'White Swirl'.

cytogenetics. The study of the genetic features of cells; notably, the study of chromosomes and genes.

dehisce (deep HISS). Natural opening of the mature anther to expose pollen; the opening of the seed pod.

diamond-dusted. Petal texture characterized by tiny, glistening highlights.

diploid. A plant with cells that have two sets of chromosomes in each somatic cell, one set contributed by each parent. Most plants occurring in nature are diploid.

division. A single rhizome of a plant with its roots and fan of leaves; the act of dividing a clump into smaller parts.

DNA, or ***deoxyribonucleic acid***. The complex chemical material within the cell that controls heredity.

durability. The ability of a flower to withstand time, sun, wind, rain, and other adverse conditions.

egg. The female gamete (germ cell), located in the ovule.

embryo. The rudimentary plant within the seed.

endosperm. A tissue in the seed that contains stored food; it surrounds and nourishes the embryo and continues to nourish the tiny seedling for the first week or more after germination.

enzyme. A protein of complex constitution, necessary for certain chemical reactions to occur in the living cell.

eupogon (<u>YOU</u> pope <u>gon</u>dola). True bearded; a true bearded iris.

falls. The three lower petals of the iris flower (botanically, the sepals), which arch downward or flare more or less horizontally.

fan. A single set of leaves rising from the rhizome.

fimbriation. A somewhat feathered, fringelike structure of the style midrib.

fungicide. A material, usually chemical, that destroys fungi.

fungus. Saprophytic or parasitic plant that reproduces from spores and by vegetative means. Of the many microscopic fungi in soil, some are harmless or beneficial, others cause molds, mildews, rusts, botrytis rot, and other diseases.

gamete (<u>gas</u> <u>MEET</u>). The male or female germ cell of a sexually reproducing organism.

garden siberians. Incorrect term, sometimes improperly used for the 28-chromosome siberian irises. Also correctly used for the cultivated siberian hybrids as distinct from the wild species.

gene pool. All the genes of a population.

gene. A unit of heredity. The portion of chromosomal DNA capable of controlling one or more characteristics.

germination. The sprouting of seeds.

glaucous. Having a whitish surface, as though powdered.

glossy. Shiny, lustrous.

grubs. Wormlike larvae of insects, such as beetles, usually found underground.

hafts. The narrower part of the falls and standards near the center of the flower. Those on the falls are usually marked with yellow in white siberians and with patterns of brown and yellow striations in darker flowers. These haft patterns may be attractive but usually are not. The signal patterns extend out on the falls from the hafts.

hue. Color; the distinctive characteristics of a color that enable it to be assigned a position in the spectrum.

hybrid. A plant that results from crossing two different species or cultivars, or from crossing a cultivar on itself.

hybridize. The act of pollinating flowers.

hypocotyl (<u>HIGH</u> <u>po</u>lar <u>co</u>llar <u>till</u>). The first part of the embryo to emerge from the germinating seed; from it, the primitive roots and leaves develop.

introduce. The formal offering of an officially registered plant for sale, as through an advertisement.

introduction. A cultivar offered for sale for the first time.

larva. The early, free-living form of an animal that changes structure markedly when it becomes an adult; for example, the caterpillar is the larva of a butterfly.

leaf. The bladelike structure that rises from the rhizome; it is especially adapted for photosynthesis and transpiration. Collectively leaves are called *foliage*.

matte. Flat texture; not glossy or velvety or diamond-dusted.

meristem. The undifferentiated plant tissue at the growing point of the plant from which new differentiated cells arise.

miniature. A small flower on a slender stalk of appropriate height. No specific measurements have been established for siberian irises as they have been for some others. In practice, however, the cultivars described as miniatures have flowers approximately 3 inches (7.5 centimeters) or less in diameter on stalks not more than 15 inches (37 centimeters) tall.

monocotyledon (mono cot it LEAf donkey). A plant that has a single seed-leaf in the embryo.

mulch. A covering for the soil. It hinders evaporation; protects plant roots from winter injury; prevents plants from heaving in winter; preserves soil texture; keeps down weeds; protects fruit and flowers from mud spattering; adds organic matter to the soil; keeps soil cool in summer; and provides dry paths in winter. Salt hay, oat straw, leaves, sawdust, shredded bark, wood chips, and many other natural materials fulfill all or some of these purposes. Plastic and aluminum sheeting are also used.

mutant. A plant in which a chemical change in DNA has occurred, or has been induced by such means as radioactive irradiation.

nematode. Any member of a phylum of nonsegmented worms, many of which are parasites of animals and plants. All that are concerned with plants are microscopic; some are harmful but many are harmless or beneficial.

ovary. The ovule-bearing structure at the base of the flower that develops into the seed pod following fertilization.

ovules. Egg-containing structures in the ovary that develop into seeds following fertilization.

parasite. A plant or animal that lives in or on an individual of another species without advantage to the host and usually doing it harm.

pedicel (PEDal it cell). The stem that connects a single flower to the main stalks or branches.

pendent. Hanging. Used to describe falls that hang and often construed as derogatory, but many pendent falls are graceful.

perianth tube. The slender tube that connects the ovary with the floral parts.

perianth. In iris flowers, collective terms for standards and falls.

pesticide. Any material used to kill pests—usually insect pests.

petals. The inner series of a flower's segments. In the iris, the standards, but often used to refer to both standards and falls. In botanical terms, the falls are the sepals.

pH. A symbol denoting the relative concentration of hydrogen ions in a solution and therefore a measure of acidity and alkalinity. Values range from pH zero to pH 14 on a logarithmic scale. A pH of 7 is neutral. Numbers below 7 indicate acidity and the lower the pH, the greater the acidity. Numbers above 7 indicate alkalinity. Most soils are between 4 and 9 on the pH scale.

pistil. The female reproductive structure of a flower. In irises it consists of ovary, styles, and stigmas.

plasmid. Extrachromosomal DNA that reproduces along with but independently of the chromosomes.

plicata. A pattern of pale color or white on the falls of an iris, in which the margins of the falls are streaked or dotted with a dark color. As yet, no siberian irises are plicatas, but the term is sometimes incorrectly applied to those with bold white areas at the base of the falls, extending out toward the tips.

pod parent. The female parent; the plant on which the seed pod will form.

pogon. A bearded iris.

pollen parent. The male parent; the plant that provides the pollen for the cross.

polyploid. A plant with cells that have more than two complete sets of chromosomes.

pupa (PEW puppy). Any insect in the nonfeeding stage of its development between the last larval and adult forms; often enclosed in a cocoon or shell-like structure.

rebloomer. An iris that has a second period of bloom occurring several months after first bloom period. See also *repeater*

register. The act of recording the name and description of an iris with the registrar of the American Iris Society.

registration. A plant named and officially registered by the registrar of the American Iris Society.

repeater. A siberian (or japanese) iris that has a second period of bloom starting two or three weeks after end of first bloom period. *Occasional repeater*: a plant that reblooms scantily and not every year. *Reliable repeater*: one that reblooms well each year if well grown. *Preferential repeater*: one whose second period of bloom is superior to the first. See also **rebloomer** and **continuing bloomer** *rhizome*. The thick, fleshy underground stem of an iris plant from which roots, leaves, and stalks arise.

roots. The extension of the plant below ground (in irises, below the rhizome) that serves both to absorb and conduct water and minerals and to anchor the plant. In irises, roots and leaves arise from the rhizome.

scape. See *stalk*

scarious. Dry, papery, not green.

sclerotia. A dormant stage in certain fungi consisting of hardened black or reddish brown masses of threads.

seed pod, or *capsule*. The elongated, round structure that develops from the ovary following fertilization and that contains the seeds.

self. A flower with all segments the same color.

self-pollination, or *selfing*. Pollinating a flower with its own pollen.

series. In the classification of irises, the major subdivisions of a subsection.

shade. A darker value of a given color, the result of its admixture with varying amounts of black. See also *tint*

sino-siberians. Inaccurate term sometimes inappropriately used for the 40-chromosome siberian irises.

signal, or *blaze*. The patterned area, usually semicircular, at the base of the falls extending out from the haft marking, with color or colors different from that of the falls.

somatic cell. A body cell in contrast to the germ cells.

spathes. The top set of bracts that, in the iris, encircle the ovary and bud but are below the open flower, which they help to support. See also *bracts*

species. Defined in various ways but usually considered to be a group of organisms (in our case, the various species of siberian irises) that interbreed and are reproductively isolated from all other such groups. Species are designated with binomials consisting of a generic name (e.g., *Iris*), the first letter of which is capitalized, and a specific epithet (e.g., *sibirica*). For greater precision in scientific literature, the binomial is followed by a name, initial, or abbreviation identifying the botanist whose description gives authority to the binomial used. For example, *Iris sibirica* L. refers to the plant described by Linnaeus.

spores. Reproductive bodies, usually single cells, produced by bacteria, fungi, and other lower plants. They are resistant to adverse conditions and can remain dormant for long periods.

stalk, or **scape**. The upright stem that rises from the rhizome and bears the flowers.

stamen. The male reproductive part of the flower, consisting of a filament and at its end, the anther, which bears the pollen grains.

standard. The upper, more or less erect petals of the iris, which usually rise above the falls.

stigma. The small, liplike structure on the undersurface of the style, close to its tip, on which pollen is deposited to effect fertilization.

stratification. The practice of storing seeds in the refrigerator at temperatures slightly above freezing for several weeks or months to enhance subsequent germination.

styles. The three firm, petal-like structures, rising from the center of the flower, that are connected with the ovary and bear the stigmas.

subseries. In taxonomic classification, a subdivision of a series. Series *Sibiricae* consists of two subseries: subseries *Sibiricae* with species and their cultivars having twenty-eight somatic chromosomes (and tetraploids derived from them) and subseries *Chrysographes* with forty somatic chromosomes and their corresponding tetraploids.

substance. The deep (as distinguished from surface) tissue characteristics of the falls and standards, which determine their firmness or flexibility and, to a large extent, the flower's form.

systemic. A term applied to pesticides, including fungicides and insecticides, that are absorbed by the plant without harm but are lethal to pests when they chew or suck sap from the plant. Systemic pesticides remain active longer than contact pesticides and when used properly are less harmful to bees and other beneficial insects.

tailored. A flower that is not ruffled or crimped.

terminal. The end of the stalk as distinct from its branches.

tetraploid. Literally, fourfold; a plant having four sets of somatic chromosomes instead of the usual two sets. See also **diploid**

texture. The surface characteristics of falls, standards, and styles.

tint. A lighter value of a given color, the result of its admixture with varying amounts of white. See also **shade**

tone. The quality or value of a given color with reference to its darkness or lightness.

triploid. A plant with three sets of somatic chromosomes. All are sterile. None have been recorded among siberian irises, but theoretically a triploid could result from crossing diploids with tetraploids.

variety. A group of individuals within a species differing sufficiently to be given a Latin varietal name usually preceded by the abbreviation "var." The use of "variety" with reference to cultivated plants is being replaced with the term "cultivar."

vector. In plant diseases, an organism—usually an insect—that carries an infectious agent from one plant to another. In gene transfer, something that carries the desired gene into the plant intended to receive it.

velvety. Texture resembling velvet.

virus. Submicroscopic infective agents that reproduce only within cells and may cause diseases in plants and animals.

wide cross. In siberian irises, a cross between plants of different species or of different subseries or series. Often they are not successful.

Index
of Names

Index
of Topics